The moon was spinning a silver mist over the ocean as Jessica slipped out of her sandals for a stroll on the beach.

"We couldn't have picked a more beautiful night," Mark said, reaching for her hand as they walked.

For years Jessica had wished on stars for a man like Mark Castleman, but she couldn't bear to be deceived a second time.

He turned to her and their eyes locked. Mark had been asking himself just how far he should go with this relationship. After the startling announcement she had made tonight, he had no idea what would happen.

"Thanks for a wonderful evening," she said, looking into his eyes.

Without thinking, he leaned down and kissed her lips.

Palisades.
Pure Romance.

FICTION THAT FEATURES CREDIBLE CHARACTERS AND
ENTERTAINING PLOT LINES, WHILE CONTINUING TO UPHOLD
STRONG CHRISTIAN VALUES. FROM HIGH ADVENTURE
TO TENDER STORIES OF THE HEART, EACH PALISADES
ROMANCE IS AN UNDILUTED STORY OF LOVE,
FROM BEGINNING TO END!

A PALISADES CONTEMPORARY ROMANCE

SEASCAPE

PEGGY DARTY

PALISADES

SEASCAPE
published by Palisades
a part of the Questar publishing family

© 1996 by Peggy Darty
International Standard Book Number: 0-88070-927-8

Cover illustration by George Angelini
Cover designed by David Carlson and
Mona Weir-Daly

Printed in the United States of America

For information:
QUESTAR PUBLISHERS, INC.
POST OFFICE BOX 1720
SISTERS, OREGON 97759

96 97 98 99 00 01 02 03 — 10 9 8 7 6 5 4 3 2 1

For the special people in my life.
Like the characters in Seascape, I wish you
the gift of forgiveness and the joy of love.

"Do not judge and you will not be judged.
Do not condemn, and you will not be condemned.
Forgive, and you will be forgiven.
…For with the measure you use, it will be measure to you."

LUKE 6:37, NIV

One

Jessica Thorne strolled along the Florida beach, gazing across the emerald water tinged with the flames of sunset. It was the end of another day, and the horizon was a luminous blend of red and gold. Jessica felt a sense of awe just looking at the seascape. She was thankful to be here, in spite of the sadness that still lingered in her heart. The month was February, and sometimes the nights were chilly. She was much warmer, though, than family and friends in other parts of the world, who suffered the winds and snows of winter.

Her dark eyes moved on to the fishing boats, edging toward the shoreline, and then she stopped walking. Far out, she could see a sailboat bobbing lazily over the gulf with bright red sails just like....

Jessica's brown eyes froze. For a moment, she was catapulted back in time and space to that horrible afternoon last fall when Blake's boat had overturned. Again, she could taste the salty ocean, hear her voice screaming against the wind, as she flailed about in the deep waves that beat and thrashed and finally swallowed Blake.

She closed her eyes, hugging her arms against her wind-breaker, hoping to still the trembling that always accompanied the memory of the accident, just months ago. She forced herself to look away, to push those torturing thoughts from her mind as she dropped her eyes to the sand at her feet.

A tiny pink shell lay beside her right tennis shoe, and she focused her attention on it, taking slow deep breaths.

"Excuse me," a male voice floated over her shoulder, "have you lost something?"

"Yes." The word rolled over her lips, an involuntary reaction.

"Can I help?"

Slowly, her dark eyes moved from the seashell up to the man who had suddenly appeared and now stood beside her. She merely stared for a moment, unable to bring herself back to the present.

"Did you drop something?" he asked helpfully, his head tilted to scan the sand at her feet. Then, seeing nothing, his eyes returned to her lovely face, and he began to wonder precisely what was wrong with her. She seemed to be in a daze. Was she ill?

Her dark lashes snapped against her olive skin, as she blinked twice, and focused on the handsome man who stood before her.

"I mean, what I've lost isn't here," she answered vaguely.

"I see," he replied, though he didn't see at all. Nevertheless, Mark Castleman was a man of sharp instincts; he was quick to sense a problem, or another person's pain. And he sensed both in this woman, who seemed reluctant to say more. He willed himself to move on, but something — he wasn't sure what — kept him rooted to the spot.

Jessica's eyes swept over him, seeing a tall man, well over six feet, with sun-streaked brown hair and sea-green eyes that looked friendly and warm. Broad shoulders tapered to a narrow waist and long legs; and it was easy to see even through his jogging suit that his muscles were well toned.

He, in turn, regarded her curiously. She was five feet seven inches, slim, almost frail, or so she seemed when she lifted a delicate hand to brush a wisp of dark hair from her cheek. Her brown eyes appeared even darker against clear white irises, and for a moment, he couldn't help staring at her. Her natural beauty was captivating; yet something else seemed to draw him.

Mark looked around, wondering if she was alone. Several yards behind them, an older couple was brandishing a metal detector, whimsically searching for treasure. The couple showed no recognition toward this woman; she had to be out for a walk on her own.

"Well," he said, pressing a broad palm against the chest of his lightweight jacket, "have a nice day."

She nodded absently as a smile touched her lips. "You too." She turned and walked away.

For a moment, he stared after her, wondering about her. Then he turned back, trying to prod himself to finish out his run. He was accustomed to looking at beautiful women; he hadn't reached thirty years of age, unattached, without being acquainted with a few. And yet....

He sneaked another glance over his shoulder, unable to squelch his curiosity.

She moved with the grace of a dancer, light and willowy, as she headed toward the far end of the beach. He tried to remember what was there — nothing much. A large, run-down house and then the park.

Forget it, he told himself. *The lady isn't interested.* Drawing a breath of salt-sprayed air, he turned and began to jog the mile and a half back to his condo.

Jessica had almost reached the steps leading up from the beach before she allowed herself a glimpse over her shoulder. She could see him a quarter of a mile away, his lean frame moving in perfect rhythm against the waves rippling onto the shoreline. Her eyes lingered on the stranger, amazed that for the first time since Blake's death she could actually look at a man, even notice whether he was attractive or not. This man jogging down the beach definitely was.

She reached out and gripped the wooden rail, wearily pulling herself up the board steps. She was making progress, she told herself; she could look at a sailboat, exactly like Blake's boat, recall the accident and not burst into tears.

And yet her tennis shoes seemed weighted with lead, and her body felt old and worn out, by the time she reached the top step and pressed the gate's latch. Stepping through the gate, her eyes scanned the gray picket fence surrounding the property. The sight of yet another feature in need of paint brought a sigh, as her thoughts returned to the project at hand.

The project, a two-story Victorian house with its half-completed cupola, was a mixed blessing. Each time she looked at the gray house with its paint-chipped trim, she saw, in her mind's eye, a paint that was the palest pink, like the inside of a seashell, with a pristine white trim to accent windows and doors.

The house had been built in the fifties by a family who owned a chunk of beach property. Obviously, they had a fondness for Victorian architecture, and thirty years ago the place must have been something to behold. It had changed hands twice since then, however, and the last owner, a Montgomery businessman, had fallen into financial difficulty. He had been forced to neglect the upkeep of his summer place here, yet he wanted to hold onto it, hoping he could recoup his losses. Unfortunately, he had not been able to keep the house from slowly sinking into disrepair before he finally had to sell it.

She walked around the side of the house, appraising it again. The foundation was sturdy, the frame boards sound and in place. From the front, the lower and upper porches invited one to sit and relax. She had installed ceiling fans already and had visions of rocking chairs and swings, made by craftsmen back in Angel Valley. Huge clay pots had already been purchased at a flea market and waited in the pantry for the petunias she would grow.

She placed hands on hips and turned to survey the view from the porch. For her guests, this would be an escape to the sea. *Seascape*.

This special dream lifted her spirits. She would continue to tackle the project step by step. She had started with paint on the inside, working her way to the outside of the house. She had to be patient and, most of all, economical. While it had presented the greatest challenge of her life, the house would be home, her home forever. The idea of putting down roots, once and for all, was like a cold drink of water to one dying of thirst.

The wind chimes tinkled delicately in the evening breeze

as she paused on the doorstep, raking sand from her tennis shoes. She tried not to panic as she thought of tourist season, which would begin in about six weeks. She was working night and day herself and had just hired a man who was both carpenter and painter to finish the outside of the house.

The screen door gave its customary creak of welcome as she entered. She walked through the house, proud of her progress so far. As the familiar smells of turpentine and paint surrounded her, Jessica felt a special empathy for the house; for she, too, needed some time and care before she could enter the mainstream of society again.

Down the beach, in a high-rise that overlooked the Gulf, Mark Castleman stood before the glass wall of his living room. His eyes were fixed on the horizon as the sun trailed scarlet ribbons across the sky. Mark was thinking this had to be the most beautiful beach in the world, with its white satin shoreline and emerald gulf. While south Florida boasted warmer weather year-round, he preferred it here in the Panhandle.

He watched an older couple, probably snowbirds, walking hand in hand along the beach, admiring the sunset. Panama City was a paradise for retired people. The prices were economical and the weather was warm and mild to those who came from places like Minnesota and Pennsylvania and Canada to loll away the winter months.

He lifted his arms over his head, stretched lazily, then dropped cross-legged to the carpet to admire the breathtaking beauty for a few minutes longer. Cupping his chin in his hands, he sat, staring thoughtfully at the ocean and enjoying the serenity that came to him now.

It was hard to imagine just how drastically his life had changed in the past year — a year that seemed to have stretched over a lifetime. A year ago, he'd been sweating the results of his bar exam, wondering if he'd make it into the legal profession after a late start. He had. And yet, he hadn't been quite ready to go to work for the prestigious Birmingham firm that offered him a job. He was restless, feeling a nagging urge to erase a question mark in his past. And the question had led him on a strange and bizarre trail, ending here.

A hunger pang hit his stomach, and he turned his thoughts toward food. There hadn't been time to stock the refrigerator when he drove over from Panama City yesterday, and now he was going to be stuck with canned soup from the cabinet if he didn't make a dash for the nearest restaurant.

He pulled up his long frame, yanking off his T-shirt as he hurried to the shower. He was craving some ice-cold, Apalachicola oysters on the half shell, and with a favorite restaurant in mind, his mouth watered and his steps quickened.

As darkness swallowed up the dying sunset, a light evening rain had begun to fall. Jessica fastened the white shutters, closing out the rainy night, and turned to face the parlor. A pale green wall surrounded her, like a wash of sea spray, reaching to a nine-foot ceiling. Beneath her feet, the hardwood floor gleamed proudly, showing off a new coat of lemon wax. The only thing missing was furniture.

When Jessica envisioned a life of luxury in Florida, as Blake had promised, she had been totally unprepared for the rambling house that awaited her. A realtor had convinced Blake the house was a "steal," and Blake had jumped right in, with typical abandon. His idea, as always, was grand scale. He would open up a bed and breakfast here, then continue with a chain of them throughout Florida. Of course he planned to hire other people to do the work while he continued to play at life. Unfortunately, his playing days had been expensive, and Jessica had been shocked to discover the extent of Blake's debts once they married.

Thrusting that memory from her mind, she wandered into the dining room and ran a hand over the buffet she had just refinished. Looking at the oak-stained wood, she felt a sense of satisfaction with her accomplishment. The previous owners had sold the furnishings with the house, leaving a few antiques mixed in with lots of junk. She had sold the junk pieces and kept the better furniture, while slowly adding other pieces from estate sales and a generous check from her parents.

Her stomach growled again, turning her thoughts toward food. She headed into the kitchen, cheered by the red accents in curtains, tablecloth, and matching cushions. Her one concession to a modern look was the black and white tiles on the floor. She couldn't resist the idea of a kitchen done in red, black, and white.

Walking to the pantry, she opened the door and surveyed the empty shelves. Could she possibly squeeze one more meal from the meager contents here? She was living on a shoestring now, with most of her money earmarked for repairs. Last night's supper had been a mayonnaise sandwich with a hint of peanut butter.

Closing the pantry door, her eyes wandered to her cheery table, meeting the jelly jar, which had been turned upside down since breakfast. Yep, there was enough jelly there for a meager sandwich, and with plenty of tea and one lone apple left in the fruit bowl, she could survive.

Thunder rumbled, and automatically her eyes lifted to the roof. Unlike some women, rain did not bother her; she loved the sound of rain. Forgetting her skimpy food supply, she turned her thoughts toward the wealth of books in the study. The previous owners had been book lovers, and their variety of books had provided her many nights of glorious escape.

She filled the kettle with water and turned on the burner. While the water heated, she hurried upstairs to put on her flannel gown and comfortable slippers. In the hallway, her eyes came to rest on the assortment of seashells arranged in a crystal bowl on the marble-topped table. She found herself thinking of the delicate little pink shell she had spotted earlier, and the pleasant man who had stopped to chat.

"Have you lost something?" he had asked.

It was a strange question, an ironic question, considering what she had actually lost…a husband and a host of youthful dreams and illusions.

She went to bed early, reading only a short while before falling asleep. Sometime in the night, however, the nightmare returned to haunt her.

She was in the water, screaming for help. A red and white cruiser approached…she squinted through wet lashes to read the name lettered on the side. BARKLEY. A man stood in the boat, staring in her direction.

"Help! Please, help us!" she screamed.

The salty water flooded her mouth and the wind snatched her voice and flung it against the sky as the boat sped away.

Two

The next morning Jessica wandered listlessly down the stairs to the kitchen. Catching sight of her reflection in the antique mirror, she winced at her swollen eyes and mussed hair. The nightmare had come again. Thank goodness, her screams had awakened her, ending the torture. After a glass of warm milk to calm her nerves, she had returned to bed, then tossed and turned for hours. It was a familiar pattern. Just before dawn she had drifted into an exhausted sleep; now she felt as though she had been moving furniture half the night.

She crossed the living room and hesitated beside the table that held her mail. She opened the drawer and withdrew a stack of letters, tied with a pink ribbon. The letters were her little treasures, notes from dear friends who had written during the difficult months, offering comfort and encouragement.

Gripping those letters, she made her way back to the kitchen, needing her morning tea. She filled the kettle and started it heating on the stove. Taking a seat at the table, she removed the ribbon and opened the first letter. Reading one of the letters was a special kind of ritual for Jessica, bringing a measure of comfort.

As she sorted through them now, bypassing those from her mother, she hesitated on the most recent one postmarked Angel Valley. Her eyes moved over the familiar scrawl on the outside of the envelope, and she fought the sting of tears. If only she could turn back the clock, have a carefree day again, just one.

She touched the ink on the return address. Mrs. Matthew Wentworth. Jessica took a deep breath, wishing she could have gone back for Laurel's wedding, but she couldn't. She just couldn't. She was glad that Laurel and Matt were married and happy; they deserved to be. But she wasn't ready to share in anyone else's joy, nor was she ready to hear anyone tell her how God would work things out for her. He hadn't done a very good job of it so far.

She scanned the letter again, smiling sadly, then returned it to the envelope. Laurel had lost her father; she knew how it felt to lose a loved one. Jessica would go through the stages of grief, Laurel warned. Thinking it over, Jessica surmised she must have reached the anger stage. She found herself resenting anyone who had never felt sorrow or pain or tasted the bitterness of disappointment and heartbreak.

Like Rosemary. Spotting Rosemary's letter as she returned Laurel's envelope to the stack, she merely sighed. She wished she didn't resent Rosemary now, but she did. She forced her mind back to happy days with Rosemary, carefree school days — cheerleading and football and picnicking in the mountains.

A tiny frown hovered between Jessica's dark brows as she retied the ribbon. Her father kept telling her she was isolating herself from her friends and family, but then Dad was the stereotypical salesman, a real extrovert who could never understand the need she and her mother felt for their periods of privacy and silence. Jessica and her mother preferred to isolate themselves while working out a problem; this was contrary to her father's way of talking through it.

She leaned against the stove, watching the steam rise from the kettle. Listlessly, she turned to the cabinet, idly running a finger over the new pine finish. With the morning sunlight streaming through the kitchen, lifting the patina to a high gloss, she felt pleased and proud of her work. It had taken days for her to remove the old varnish and sand down the cabinets. But her hard work had been rewarded by mounting satisfaction.

She heard a car engine out in the driveway and turned to open the wooden shutters over the kitchen sink.

"Oh no," she moaned softly, then bit her lip, ashamed of herself. The familiar green van was pulling into the drive beside her black economy car. Blake's parents, having retired in Destin, thirty minutes away, took it upon themselves to come calling twice a week, checking on her. At times, it was a strain to be polite, to answer their questions respectfully, yet she always felt sympathetic about their loss of an only child. Her main concern, however, was the way they regarded her as replacement for Blake. She closed her eyes, trying to summon all her mental energy, before dashing a hand over her hair and hurrying to the door.

Since their early retirement, both enjoyed casual dress; they always looked as though they had just come off the golf course. Most of the time they had. Today, both Sue and Mel Vandercamp were wearing tan jumpsuits.

"Hi, girl, how are you?" Sue reached out, taking Jessica into her arms for a quick hug. "Thought you were going to come down for dinner one evening?"

Jessica wrapped her arms around the little woman, who was scarcely five feet tall, with short blonde hair and lively blue eyes.

"I was just too busy, Sue. Sorry."

Sue held Jessica at arm's length, scanning her daughter-in-law from head to toe with the usual curiosity. "You've lost another pound or two," she observed.

"Sue, leave the poor girl alone," Mel scolded, peering down from his six-foot-four vantage point. "She'll hate to see us coming if you don't quit smothering her!"

Although a wry grin played over his heavy features, Jessica suspected he was testing her, for beneath bushy brows his keen gray eyes measured her reaction.

"Don't be silly," Jessica replied, forcing a smile. "Come in the kitchen, I was just having tea."

"When does the painter start on the outside?" Mel inquired, wandering into the hallway to poke around.

"Next week," Jessica replied, praying he wouldn't make another offer to come help.

Sue turned to her husband. "Mel, why don't you — "

"Please," Jessica touched Sue's arm, hoping to ward off a stream of suggestions, "don't worry about it. I've already hired someone to do the work. Besides, you two have better things to do."

Mel ducked under the archway to the kitchen. "Every penny counts, little girl. Just keep that in mind."

"Honestly," Sue sank into the chair, "I just don't know what Blake was thinking of, buying this albatross."

"I'm beginning to like it here," Jessica replied cheerfully as she placed china cups on the table for the older couple.

The Vandercamps knew, of course, that Jessica had been distraught to learn that the house Blake had bought was not as "ready" for a bed and breakfast as he had boasted. When he had acknowledged that a "few" minor repairs were needed, he had made the understatement of the century, in Jessica's opinion.

Mel snorted. "If Mother knew the money she left Blake went for this monstrosity...."

Jessica avoided his eyes, grateful she had chosen to protect Mel and Sue from a shattered image of their only son. Blake's death had broken their hearts; there was no point in adding more pain at this stage in their lives. Blake had almost depleted his grandmother's savings by the time he bought the house; the remaining mortgage had been a revelation from which Jessica was reeling to this day. Still, he had put down just enough to get financing from the number-one loan shark in the area.

Jessica looked up, meeting two pairs of curious eyes. She realized they were waiting for her to respond to Mel's comment about the house.

She forced a smile. "To be honest, the work here has been therapy for me," Jessica poured tea. "After Mom came down and spent that first month, showing me how to paint and refinish —"

"Well, you've worked a miracle," Sue said, shaking her head. "It wouldn't be my cup of tea, so to speak." She and Mel both laughed at her pun.

Jessica smiled politely at the couple as she joined them at the round oak table, smoothing a wrinkle from the red linen cloth. She did get lonely, and when she looked at Sue, Blake's eyes seemed to stare back at her. Sometimes it was a comfort, sometimes it brought pain. They sipped their tea together in silence, until her father-in-law voiced the predictable question.

"Have you talked to the attorney this week?"

"Mel, don't start," Sue begged, blinking rapidly as though fighting back tears.

Jessica dropped her eyes. Why did they always have to get back to the accident, Blake's death, and the possibility of a lawsuit? Why couldn't they, for once, just have a pleasant conversation?

"Jessica knows we're just concerned," Mel explained hoarsely, for the subject always brought tension and bitterness.

Jessica drew a deep breath. "Mel, Mr. Barkley is a very powerful man and —"

"He chose to leave you and Blake out in the water." Mel's finger jabbed the air, pointing toward the ocean. "If only he had stopped, Blake would still be alive...." His voice broke and he bolted out of the chair. Turning his back, he stood before the window, staring out, trying to hide his tears.

Sue cleared her throat. "You said Barkley's real estate company holds a small mortgage on this house." Sue's reminder was something Jessica wished to forget, and she almost choked on her tea at the word *small*.

"We've heard such horror stories about the man," Sue continued, glancing at her husband's stiff back. "Even though he owns half the houses and condos in this area, he apparently has a heart of stone. The banker in Destin told us Barkley is completely ruthless, overcharging, then repossessing —"

Jessica closed her eyes, unable to bear the thought. Her

head had begun to throb, as always, when the subject turned to Barkley, for he had been the source of the nightmares that plagued her.

"I'll look into it next week," she promised, wondering if she had the strength to do that.

"Don't you want Mel to handle it?" Sue reached across the table, squeezing Jessica's hand.

"No," she replied firmly, looking Sue straight in the eye.

"I've been thinking of paying that scoundrel a call," Mel burst out as he turned back to face Jessica.

Jessica looked worriedly at her father-in-law. His cheeks were flushed, signaling a possible rise in his blood pressure, a constant source of worry for Sue.

"Calm down, honey." Sue fidgeted with a short curl above her ear. "Let's not worry about it. Jessica's attorney is being paid to worry. Let him earn his money."

Mel took a long deep breath. "Well, I think the law firm you chose is the best one," he said quietly. "I called a dozen people —"

Jessica could see he was making an attempt to be reassuring. "I know, and I'm sure they're very competent," Jessica replied. "In the meantime, I have to think of my work here. Tourist season is only six weeks away."

"That's right," Sue looked back at Mel, her tone carrying an unspoken reprimand. "We don't need to be discussing this. Jessica, did I tell you we've found a new driving range?"

Jessica suppressed a sigh of relief as the subject switched to golf, their favorite hobby. Soon the conversation was back to normal, and eventually Mel glanced at his wrist watch.

"Speaking of golf," he looked at his wife, "our tee time is one o'clock."

Sue's blue eyes lingered on Jessica. "I just feel so guilty leaving you all alone down here. This strip of beach seems a bit remote to me. Don't you want to come stay with us for a while?"

Jessica shook her head. "I'm just fine, really. I've always been a bit of a loner, so I'm content."

The couple exchanged a glance, then looked at her again. *A loner?* She was pleasant and warm, but then they were still getting to know her. They had met her only once before the wedding when Blake had brought her to meet the family. So much had happened.

"And besides," Jessica smiled, "I'm getting a new boarder."

Both faces registered surprise, then alarm.

"Her name is Wilma and she's from Canada," Jessica explained patiently. "She and her husband enjoyed vacationing in Florida. He died last summer, and she decided to spend the winter here. Of course, she's on a limited income, so she decided to pick up a part-time job, to keep her busy as much as anything. She says she loves to keep house, and Seascape will give her something to do."

Sue looked at her husband, hesitation clear in her expression.

Since both tended toward skepticism, Jessica knew that her new boarder would be a matter of concern to both Sue and Mel. She realized she had better tell them more about Wilma, before they took it upon themselves to check the poor woman out.

"She's a friend of Mrs. Tillotson," Jessica spoke slowly, deliberately.

Sue frowned. "Mrs. Tillotson?"

"The manager of the Wayfarer just down the road. Mrs.

Tillotson assures me that Wilma is a wonderful lady."

"Well…," Mel echoed his wife's response, then began to nod. "We would feel better about you having someone in the house with you. I guess that will be a good arrangement," he decided, and with that Sue began to smile and nod as well.

The couple exchanged another tight embrace with Jessica before they rushed off to their golf game. Jessica waved bravely then quickly closed the door. Moaning with relief, she pressed her head against the door frame and wondered how much longer she could force herself to be polite when at times she wanted to snap at them. Of course, she couldn't do that.

Still, every day was becoming a major struggle, and her nerves were beginning to wear thin. She wandered back to the kitchen and finished her tea, staring solemnly at the pantry. She simply had to restock the larder. It would be embarrassing when Wilma arrived and discovered that even a stray bug would get malnutrition in this kitchen.

Resigned to the task, she headed back upstairs and pulled a pair of khaki slacks and a long-sleeved white blouse from the closet. Time to begin another day.

Last night's storm still lingered in the morning breeze, and Mark felt wonderful as he hopped into his white Corvette and cranked the engine. A weekend at the condo had done wonders for his morale, and he began to hum as he drove out of the parking lot. Waving to the security guard at the gate, he turned onto the main thoroughfare and headed toward the little shopping center several miles away.

Armed with a plastic bag of coupons and a printout of the grocery list, Jessica entered the store. She had set up her computer and printer in the study, now serving as an office, and created a master list for her groceries. If she was going to run a bed and breakfast, she told herself, she had better be organized from the outset. Being organized was important to Jessica; in fact, it had been a major source of difficulty with Blake, during their brief, turbulent marriage. Blake was impulsive and impatient, and their opposite natures had played havoc with the relationship.

The electronic doors swung open before her, and she entered the brightly lit store and looked around. By the wall clock, it was only 9:00 A.M., which explained why the store was half empty. She grabbed a cart and headed toward the produce where a sleepy young man was sipping coffee from a foam cup while restocking sacks of oranges.

Although she rarely drank coffee, its enticing aroma drifted from his cup, and she hurried to take advantage of the free coffee offered to customers at a help-yourself stand. She filled a cup, added sugar and creamer, then moved on. The coffee was fresh and tasted wonderful to her, offsetting the chill of the morning's breeze after last night's rain.

Consulting her list, she moved around the produce, carefully selecting the items she needed. Taking another sip of coffee, she turned a corner, then suddenly remembered she had bypassed the bread section. She glanced back over her shoulder. Had they restocked fresh bread on the shelves this morning?

The shopping cart kept moving, though, and it was the clanging jolt, followed by the hot coffee down her white blouse, that threw her into shock.

"Oh, I'm sorry!"

The driver of the cart she had struck was rapidly approaching, as Jessica pulled her eyes from the wet mess on her chest to the tall man she had seen at the beach yesterday.

"I'm so sorry," he repeated, his hand extended to steady her buggy. "Are you okay?" He was staring at her soggy blouse as a clerk rushed up with a cloth.

"Yes, I'm fine," she mumbled, while her cheeks burned with embarrassment as she reached for the cloth and all her coupons went sailing to the floor.

The stranger turned his attention to scooping up a handful of coupons. It was a classic case of adding insult to injury, Jessica decided, as he made a grab for a ten cent discount on toilet tissue.

"Here you go." He handed her the coupons, which she quickly deposited in her purse. "Let me take that," he added, removing the empty cup from her hand. The hot coffee had trickled down her arm and hand as well, and now Jessica, the handsome stranger, and even the clerk were all staring at the red splotches on her arm, and then the brown stain on her blouse as she used the cloth to its best advantage.

Her eyes shot back to the stranger who was handing the cup to the gawking clerk.

"Could you toss this, please?" he asked, mobilizing the clerk at last. "I am sorry," he repeated, looking down at Jessica.

She swallowed. "It was my fault."

"There's a dry cleaning shop next door," he continued smoothly. "I'm sure they can loan you a blouse while this one is being cleaned."

"Oh, that isn't necessary," she began, then glanced down

at the front of her blouse and saw that it was quite necessary. She couldn't wander around the store with this huge stain, nor could she put up with the wet blouse much longer. "I...I'll just go home."

"Please," he insisted. "It was my fault; I insist you let me make amends."

"But —"

Before she could get her head straight, or summon the physical strength to resist, he had gently managed to steer her out of the store, to the dry cleaning shop next door.

Jessica was still befuddled as he explained the situation to the friendly clerk in the shop.

"I just happen to have a fresh blouse that was never claimed," the clerk said. "You're welcome to it, although I think it will be a bit large," she said, as her eyes ran over Jessica's slim frame.

"It doesn't matter," Jessica replied, still feeling embarrassed. As the clerk disappeared, Jessica looked back at her companion. "I really should go on home."

"And you can. But why not put on a dry blouse first?" His open smile was quite disarming. What he said made perfect sense.

She looked up at him, confused by his kindness. He was a hard man to refuse, for he seemed to take charge before she could stop him. And yet he meant well. She sensed that. A reluctant smile crossed her lips.

"I really do appreciate you being so helpful."

"My pleasure. By the way, I'm Mark Castleman."

She extended her hand. "Jessica Thorne." She had gone back to her maiden name since discovering the extent of Blake's indebtedness.

"Here you go, ma'am." The helpful clerk extended a large floral blouse. "I've put a rush on your blouse; it should be ready within the hour. You could get a cup of coffee at that wonderful bakery next door. Or you may not want any more coffee," she added with a wry grin.

Jessica shook her head. "I may never want any more coffee. The funny thing is, I don't normally drink the stuff." She accepted the blouse and began to giggle, which was out of character, but the entire incident was becoming comical.

"Not a blouse you'd purchase for yourself?" Mark asked, amused, as they both stared at the huge blue and green flowers on the size forty blouse.

"Definitely not," she said, as the giggling gave way to deep laughter.

"You can change in there," the clerk indicated a dressing area in the back of the shop.

Behind the curtained dressing room, Jessica buttoned up the blouse, which stretched halfway to her knees. She saw in the mirror that she looked ridiculous, but what did it matter? The blouse was warm and dry, and she should be grateful. She swallowed her pride and emerged from the dressing room as Mark was pressing some money into the clerk's hand.

"In an hour," she replied, glancing back at Jessica.

Mark's eyes swept over her, crinkling at the corners, but at least he kept a straight face when he spoke. "Let's see what the bakery has to offer."

Jessica hesitated. "What about your shopping?"

He shrugged. "I had just begun. And I have plenty of time."

Jessica decided she couldn't argue with that, and she

might enjoy making a friend. There had been so little time; furthermore, she hadn't wanted to be with anyone, but Mark Castleman was pleasant and fun and...well, why not?

When they stepped into the bakery next door, a marvelous smell of cinnamon wafted to greet them. Jessica swallowed, trying to ignore a pang of hunger. Looking around, she saw that at this early hour the bakery was practically deserted, with the exception of two older women seated at a table in the rear. When Jessica and Mark entered, both women did a double take, as their eyes lingered on the blouse Jessica was wearing.

Jessica turned to Mark, whispering under her breath. "I think those ladies are envying my blouse."

"Oh, I'm sure!" Mark said with mock seriousness, casting a glance toward the back table before the ladies quickly turned around. He grinned down at Jessica, who was biting her lip in an effort not to start giggling again. "What'll you have?" he asked, as they eyed the fresh muffins being put into the showcase.

"So many choices," Jessica sighed, wishing she could have one of each to take home. She'd have to remember this bakery once she opened the bed and breakfast.

"I'll have a blueberry muffin and orange juice," Mark decided.

"The same for me," she said, keeping it simple.

She gathered up napkins, straws and plastic forks as Mark paid the bill and brought their tray of goodies. She chose a table by the window that overlooked the parking lot and shopping center.

"Well, I needed breakfast anyway," he said, as they settled into their chairs.

"Me too," she smiled, inserting a straw into the carton of orange juice.

They ate in silence for a few minutes before he touched the napkin to his mouth and looked at her with mild curiosity.

"Do you live here or are you just vacationing?"

"I live here. And you?"

"Both. Actually, I live over in town but I'm staying in a condo on the beach."

She nodded, thinking that's where he had come from, or was going to, when they met on the beach.

"How long have you been here?" he asked, as his eyes sneaked down to her hands. He had taken note, when he first saw her, that she was not wearing a wedding ring, but he saw the gold band on her right hand and wondered what that meant.

"I came in August," she answered, her eyes lowered to her muffin.

She suddenly looked sad, he thought, and wondered whether it had something to do with what she had left behind or what she had discovered here.

"Do you like the beach?" he asked, feeling his way along. He was remembering how she had seemed so lost in thought when he first saw her walking along the shore.

She turned her large brown eyes to him, and Mark found himself suddenly lost in their velvety depths. He had to give himself a mental shake to follow what she was saying.

"...adjustment at first, but now I don't think I'll want to live anywhere else. I love the ocean."

He nodded in agreement. "So do I. I was raised in a city, Birmingham, Alabama, and I came here with my family during school breaks. It was fun, but I always thought I'd get tired of the beach. So far I haven't; in fact, I really enjoy it."

She tilted her head back, regarding him thoughtfully. "What brings you here now?"

He hesitated. "It's a long story, actually. I came with the idea of being here only a short time, but I'm thinking of taking a job and staying on for a while."

It was hard for him to talk about his life now; most people couldn't relate to what he had done.

"Do you jog every day?" she asked, reaching for her juice. He smiled. So she had been more observant yesterday than she had appeared.

"Yeah, I love it. I played baseball and basketball in high school; then in college I took up track."

"Where did you go to school?"

"Sanford."

She nodded. "I hear that's a very good school. I went to Murray State in Kentucky."

"You're from Kentucky?" he asked, interested.

She pushed aside her empty plate and reached for the napkin. "My parents moved around a lot; we ended up in Louisville right before I entered college."

He smiled, looking out at the parking lot which had begun to fill up with morning shoppers. "I lived in the same house, on the same street in Vestavia Hills all my life. I always thought we needed a change to break the monotony."

"Then I'd like to have swapped places with you!" She stared out the window for a moment, then looked back at him. "I guess other people's lives always seem more interesting." A smile played over her lips, and he noticed the tiny dimple in her right cheek. "Or that was the case for me, growing up. Every time I made friends and started liking the house we were in, Dad's company transferred him. He was a salesman for a pharmaceutical company.

"Mother never seemed to mind, but my brother and I hated it. I think all our moving around was what prompted Chad to marry right out of high school and settle in Knox-ville in the landscaping business. I suspect Kathy — that's his wife — wishes he were more adventurous, but," she shrugged, "I guess we are all products of our upbringing."

Mark nodded, listening, and suddenly his green eyes were very serious. Looking at him, Jessica saw the change and wondered just what he was thinking.

"So, does your family still live in Birmingham?" she asked.

"Yeah, and I miss them. My sister has lived in Texas since she married two years ago. I'm an uncle," he grinned. "Twins."

"Great. What are their names?"

"Mike and Molly. They're ten months old and about to drive Felicia crazy. Mom went to Texas for a couple of weeks to help out; when she returned, she went straight to bed and stayed there for forty-eight hours." He chuckled, bringing a gleam of humor to his eyes. "Even though she was exhausted, I know Mom went crazy over her grandchildren."

Jessica listened, smiling as he spoke. She thought it must be wonderful to come from a stable family who had lived in the same neighborhood all those years.

"Twins," she repeated, thinking of her brother. "My brother and sister-in-law say they aren't ready for kids."

"Yeah, I sometimes wonder if I'm cut out for it."

As her eyes slipped over his features she couldn't help

noticing how handsome he was. She took a deep breath, glancing at the wall clock.

They had another thirty minutes before the blouse was ready. Suddenly she felt anxious about the conversation; what could she talk about now? She supposed this was a good opportunity for her to get back in the habit of conversation, something she'd need to do if she expected to be a good hostess.

She cleared her throat. "I'm opening a bed and breakfast next month."

"Really?" He leaned back in the chair, looking at her curiously. "Who's helping you?"

She took a deep breath, folding her hands on the table. "I'm doing this project alone."

He arched an eyebrow, thinking it was quite a feat for someone so young. His eyes ran over her face, noting her smooth skin, the absence of wrinkles. She couldn't be more than early twenties; maybe twenty-four.

"I'm impressed," he said, staring at her.

"Don't be until I pull it off! The place had some major repairs and needed paint, both inside and out. I'm really just getting started."

"This is amazing! Where is your place?"

"The end of Driftwood Drive. Last house on the right. Actually, it's the only house down at that end of the beach."

He nodded, trying to remember. He had only driven down there once when he was lost and needed to turn around. He didn't remember much about the house, aside from the fact that it was a large Victorian that needed work. He nodded slowly. "I think I know where it is." He glanced at the wall clock. "Look, could I interest you in dinner tonight? I'll be going back into Panama City tomorrow and…well, I'm really craving some good seafood tonight. What do you say?"

It would be difficult to refuse a free meal, or the opportunity to get to know Mark Castleman better. But was it too soon after Blake's death to start dating again? As she toyed with the idea, he leaned forward, peering into her eyes.

"I didn't ask but…are you involved with someone?" Again, he was staring at her ring finger.

She shook her head. "No. And yes, I'd like to have dinner with you tonight."

He grinned, glad he had asked. She was a beautiful woman who seemed nice and certainly more serious-minded than any of the flighty females he had taken out lately. He sensed a bit of a mystery about her, but perhaps he could clear that up over dinner.

"Shall I pick you up around six? That way we can enjoy the sunset on the gulf while we eat."

She nodded. "That's fine. And we have now managed to kill an hour," she was checking the wall clock. "I can't thank you enough."

He shook his head. "No thanks are necessary unless they're mine. There wasn't a crumb in the cabinets at the condo, and now I've had a tasty breakfast and a good laugh, if you don't mind my saying so." His eyes dropped to the huge floral blouse and they both began to laugh.

"So have I," she said, nodding.

They stood and pushed their chairs under the table. Jessica glanced toward the couple entering the building, and saw that they, too, were fascinated by her huge floral blouse.

"I never knew people were so fashion-conscious," she

whispered as they walked back out onto the sidewalk and felt the warm sunshine on their faces.

"Yeah, I guess we're all pretty critical." He glanced around at the people headed toward the grocery. "There was a lady in our church who used to wear funny hats. My friend, Tommy Rutherford, and I were always poking fun. Earned me a good spanking after I got home."

Jessica's dark eyes slid back to him. She was not surprised at his reference to church. He had certainly played the Good Samaritan with her.

They had reached the front door of the dry cleaners, and she turned and put up her hand. "You don't need to come in. You probably need to finish your shopping."

He nodded, shoving his hands in the pockets of his jeans. "Be careful," he warned, "and I'll pick you up at six."

"Right." She smiled, then hurried inside, wondering if she had done the right thing, agreeing to have dinner with him. Maybe she shouldn't complicate her life with a man, but he had been so nice to her that it would have seemed rude, or certainly awkward, to refuse.

Accepting her clean blouse and hurrying to change, she realized this was the first time she had felt lighthearted in a very long while.

Three

At the same hour, a man with dark hair and thick-lensed glasses slumped in a chair opposite the desk of Dr. Bill Shackleford. The room was heavy with silence, broken only by the older man's heavy breathing.

"Mr. Barkley, I've been practicing medicine for almost twenty years," Bill Shackleford was saying. "The only time I hate my work is when I have to tell a patient what I've just told you."

The doctor's face mirrored his concern as he looked into the dark eyes of the man who had always seemed so abrupt, so uncaring. Lately, Bill had noticed another side to Jack Barkley, confirming the rumor that he had somehow had a change of heart. Bill Shackleford's receptionist even remarked that Mr. Barkley seemed like a pretty nice man, which was a stark departure from his image as a ruthless, self-centered millionaire. Barkley never seemed to care about the doctor or his family. Today, however, the doctor noticed a distinct difference in the man's attitude. He kept squinting at the family photograph on Bill's desk.

"How old are your two sons?" Barkley asked quietly.

Bill glanced at the recent photograph of his wife Lisa and their two sons.

"Six and eight." Bill smiled proudly as he looked at his sons. Then, as his eyes returned to Barkley's ashen face, he felt a stab of pity.

"How long do I have?" Barkley asked abruptly. His voice made a grating sound in the room where only the ticking of the desk clock broke the silence of a quiet Saturday morning. Normally, the office was closed, but the doctor had made an exception, under the circumstances.

Bill Shackleford's eyes slid back to the older man, wondering exactly how to phrase the bad news.

"Just the truth," Barkley snapped, adjusting his glasses to peer into the doctor's face. "Don't waste your time or mine with false promises. You've already told me surgery isn't an option."

The doctor nodded slowly. "Every case is different. I can only give you the benefit of what the average scenario would be, given the extent of —"

"The cancer," Barkley finished for him. His ruddy skin sagged over large features and downturned lips. Behind the glasses, the dark eyes, weary and despondent, sat in pockets of loose skin. Bill thought the man looked a decade older than his sixty-one years.

Bill took a deep breath and gave him the truth. "You might live six months."

Barkley came slowly to his feet. He was not a tall man, scarcely five feet eight inches, and had been overweight for ten years. A drastic weight loss in recent months was unflattering to the cut of his Brooks Brothers suit.

"I appreciate your honesty," Barkley replied, his voice edged with the rasp from years of bourbon and Havana cigars.

"Mr. Barkley, shall I schedule—"

"No!" He dismissed the question with a toss of the hand as he walked slowly toward the door. "I'll phone you."

"Good-bye," Bill called after him, sinking back into his chair, staring at the closing door.

Downstairs, in front of the professional building that housed the doctors' offices, a black limousine waited at the curb. The engine purred smoothly, keeping the air conditioner at a comfortable level for the man who would soon occupy the backseat. A uniformed driver sat behind the wheel, his head nodding slowly in rhythm to the music on the radio.

Beneath the dark cap, his eyes slid to the revolving glass doors, through which his employer was emerging. The chauffeur snapped to attention, switching to the local news and weather station, Barkley's personal choice. Then he hopped out of the car and sprinted around to open the back door.

Stealing a glance at Barkley, the chauffeur was momentarily taken aback. Mr. Barkley looked as though someone had just knocked the breath out of his body; his face was an odd shade of gray, and he moved as though he were ancient. A visit to the doctor didn't appear to have helped Mr. Barkley's chest cold; no sir, not one bit.

Without a word, Barkley sank into the beige leather cushions of the backseat and stared glumly down the boulevard. The chauffeur closed the door gently, then dashed to hop in behind the wheel.

"Home, sir?" he asked gently.

Barkley removed his glasses and rubbed his eyes. "No, I want to go to my attorney's office."

The chauffeur swallowed his surprise, not daring to question his employer. The years had taught him well. Adjusting the rear view mirror, then checking the traffic, he slid the car back onto the boulevard and headed toward the sleek high-rise several blocks away.

Mark tried to conceal his surprise as he stood on the wide front porch, tapping lightly on Jessica's front door. He crossed his arms over his fresh yellow polo shirt, and idly checked the condition of his tan slacks. When she said she had to redo the place, she wasn't kidding, he thought worriedly, as his eyes strayed back over the rough exterior, desperately in need of paint.

Suddenly, the door opened and he caught his breath as he looked at her. Her dark hair glistened, as though she had just shampooed it, and her face was lovely, even though she had added only a bit of mascara and a pale gloss on her lips.

"Hi," she smiled.

"Hi." Mark's eyes sailed over her head as he fought off the strong attraction he felt each time he looked at her. She was a pretty woman, yet it was a natural kind of beauty, the kind that mattered to him. She was wearing a long floral skirt and another white shirt, that accented her dark hair and eyes.

"Come in," she said, pushing the screen door back.

As soon as he stepped into the foyer, the entire mood of the house changed, and for a moment, he could only stare, amazed at the abrupt change from exterior to interior.

44

"Wow," he said, as his eyes traveled over the soft creamy walls, adorned with simple prints or nice reproductions.

"Looks quite different from the outside, doesn't it?" Her dark eyes glowed with amusement, and he was relieved to see that she didn't take offense easily.

"You must have been working hard," he said, shaking his head.

"I have. Would you like a tour? More furniture is coming this week, and I have lots of plans. But some of those plans will have to wait."

He was looking up at the ceilings, which appeared to be in good condition. "How old is this house?"

"It was built in the fifties by a couple who were fond of Victorian architecture. So am I. It's actually very well built, with sturdy foundations and solid walls. I'm trying to keep the Victorian mood while updating it enough to make it a practical bed and breakfast. Fortunately, each bedroom had a bath, and that's crucial to a bed and breakfast."

As she led him from room to room, showing off the simple yet distinctive lines, Mark's amazement grew.

"This is great. Your guests are going to love it."

She sighed. "I hope so." Since he had shown so much interest, she told him the rest of her plans — the front porch swings, the flowers, the cupola to be completed on top. "Do you think the cupola is too farfetched?" she asked tentatively.

"No, I like it. I assume you've been to Seaside."

She laughed. "Of course! Where do you think I'm getting my ideas? I love what they've done down there, building Victorian cottages and adding little cupolas on the roofs."

They were walking around the upstairs hall when suddenly he stopped, staring at a blank wall.

"Mom has a painting that would be perfect there," he said, glancing back at her. "She redecorated not long ago, and the last time I saw the painting it was in a back closet."

Jessica looked at him, wondering how to respond.

"I think you should have it. If you want it, I mean. It's not a valuable painting, but it certainly fits the mood here. You may have seen it; two little girls are sitting in the sand dunes, staring at the sunset."

"I know the one! And believe it or not, I looked at it for a long time at a shop over in Panama City." She named the artist and Mark nodded.

"Yep, that's it."

"Let me buy it," she began then caught herself, wondering if he took Visa.

Mark shook his head. "No." He stared at the wall for a long time. "I think my mother would be pleased to see it here." He turned to face her. "I'll have Mom ship it down."

"Oh, no. That's too much trouble."

"Well," he shrugged, "maybe we can work something out. My parents can be a guest at your bed and breakfast sometime."

"Well…yes, of course. That's a good trade-off for me. I hope it suits your mother."

He grinned. "She's always glad to help out. They spend a month each summer doing mission work someplace. They ship a ton of stuff to those mission sites, so she's accustomed to giving things away."

Listening, Jessica thought about how nice his folks must be. "A mission trip? I recall a pastor and his wife going on summer mission trips; that was back in Tennessee."

He nodded. "My folks are strong Christians."

Jessica looked at him curiously. "And you?"

He shrugged. "Not as devout as they are, but I try to be a decent guy." He grinned at her again.

"You already played the Good Samaritan today," she teased. While she was trying to be humorous, there was an edge to her tone, and she wondered if he noticed. This talk of religion was making her nervous.

"Hey," he glanced at his watch. "Our reservations are for this very minute. We'd better scoot, as much as I hate to leave."

She grabbed her small clutch purse and dropped in the house key. "Sorry to detain you with my lengthy tour."

"Not at all. I'm the one who's held us up by insisting on seeing the house. It's great." He glanced back over his shoulder as they walked out the front door, and Jessica quickly locked up.

"I have a painter coming in the morning to do the outside," she said, staring glumly at the peeling paint on the boards beside the door. "I hope he's reliable. I'm in a push for time."

"Can I help? I've never had a paintbrush in my hand, but I'll try almost anything once."

She turned to look at him, shaking her head in amazement. "I can't believe you're offering! I'm not accustomed to a man willing to jump in and do the work."

He wondered who she using as a comparison, but he kept the question to himself as they walked out to his car.

"My father is a salesman who, to my knowledge, has never driven a nail in the wall," Jessica continued. "Mom was always on a search for the local handyman, or else she did it herself."

47

"Then you must have acquired some of her skill," he said, opening the door for her. Again, he noted how gracefully she moved, slipping into the front seat, crossing her legs at the ankles. She was wearing white sandals, and he could see that her feet were as slender and graceful as her hands.

"I do have a bit of her skill, but not nearly enough," she answered lightly. Her brown eyes looked huge in her thin face, and although she had a nice figure, Mark noted, she would probably look better if she weighed a few more pounds.

He got in and cranked the engine. "It's really quiet down here, isn't it? Do you get lonely, or frightened?"

She shook her head. "No, I enjoy the peace and quiet."

Glancing at her as he turned the wheel and pulled back onto the road, it struck him again how different she was from anyone he had ever dated. So many girls had flaunted their independence, yet underneath their facade, they were clinging vines, wanting men to do everything for them after all. This lady was feminine and soft-spoken; still, she had taken on a huge job and managed it well.

"I still find it hard to believe you've done all this on your own. Did your parents come down to help out?"

"My parents came last fall, and Mom stayed on for a month." Jessica hesitated. She hated to spoil the evening by talking about Blake and the tragedy, but at some point she would have to tell him. He had been honest with her; it was time for her to tell him why she was here.

Jessica drew a deep breath, deciding there was no point in delaying it. She hated deceit, and if she didn't explain her situation now, he was likely later on to think she had held something back.

"Mark, there's something I haven't told you.…"

He steered the car onto the main thoroughfare leading to a popular seafood restaurant, and yet every nerve was alerted to her tone of voice. He sensed she was about to say something very important about her life, and he found himself more than a little eager to know what it was. Her eyes held the look of someone who had felt deep pain, and yet she seemed to be reasonably happy.

"I was married when I first came here," she said. The words were spoken slowly, deliberately.

Mark shot a glance at her face and saw that she suddenly looked pale; she had closed her eyes.

"He drowned last fall."

Mark caught his breath. "I'm sorry! That must have been terrible for you."

"Yes, it was." She opened her eyes. "We were going to redo the house together."

"I see," he said, turning into the restaurant. This explained a lot to him, added some missing pieces to the puzzle of this woman who intrigued him so much. They had reached the restaurant and he pulled into a parking space and cut the engine. Then he turned on the seat and regarded her solemnly. "Jessica, I really am sorry."

She nodded. "Thank you."

For a moment their eyes held, and as Jessica looked at him, she sensed he really did care about what had happened to her. She was glad she had told him.

Laughter flowed from behind the car as a couple strolled by, teasing, kissing.

Mark took a deep breath. "Shall we go inside?"

"Sure." She smiled again, then reached for her purse.

As they entered the rustic restaurant, with fishing motifs displayed on driftwood walls, a hostess rushed up, smiling at Mark.

"Could we get a table by the window?" he asked.

"You're in luck," she nodded, leading them back to a private area with a spectacular view of the gulf.

As Mark held her chair, Jessica took a seat and glanced appreciatively at the gorgeous sunset turning the blue water to liquid flame. She was glad she had never come here with Blake. There would be no unpleasant memories to haunt her, just the opportunity to make friends with a man who had been very nice to her.

"What'll you have?" he asked, as the menus were placed before them.

Jessica looked over the many choices, then decided on char-grilled shrimp.

"Sounds good," Mark nodded. "I think I'll have the grouper. And could you please bring us one of those cheese samplers for an appetizer?"

They ordered iced teas, then smiled across the table at one another.

"Do you like to fish?" she asked.

Mark arched an eyebrow. "As a matter of fact, I do. I'm a little surprised that you would even ask. Most women aren't into fishing."

Jessica smiled. "I am. My happiest years were spent up in the Smokies. I use to fish with Dad in those mountain streams up there."

"The Smokies? I love that area."

"We lived in a little community called Angel Valley. I doubt that you've ever heard of it. It's tucked into the mountains, way off the beaten path, but less than an hour from Gatlinburg."

"Sounds wonderful. Do you ever go back?"

Jessica shook her head. "No, I haven't visited since I got married." She glanced at Mark. "I wanted to be married in the little church there, because Angel Valley was the only place we'd lived in that really felt like home."

He was studying her thoughtfully. "How long ago was that?"

"Last July."

He looked into her eyes, looked away, looked back again. "Then…you weren't married long when…," his voice trailed as he stirred his tea.

"We had only been married for three months."

His eyes shot back to her, and Jessica realized that he was brimming with questions that he was too polite to ask.

"It was a whirlwind courtship," she explained. "We met at the Kentucky Derby. He had come down from Boston with friends." She frowned as her fork picked idly at the shrimp. "I'm normally a pretty sensible person."

"Yes, I can see that."

"But somehow I got swept off my feet and married him without really knowing him." She fell silent, unwilling to say anything against Blake. It didn't seem fair or right.

Mark watched her carefully, trying to figure out the rest of the story. She certainly wasn't starry-eyed when she mentioned the man she had married. What had happened, he wondered? He pressed his lips together, telling himself he mustn't pry, and yet he felt himself strongly attracted to this woman. Before he let himself get involved, he had a right to know more.

"You said you married him without really knowing him. Does that mean your marriage wasn't…," his voice trailed as he searched for the right words. Maybe he was being too personal.

"Marriage is always an adjustment," she said quietly. "And I was devastated by the boating accident."

Boating accident. Mark racked his brain, trying to recall the newspapers he had read on his frequent visits here back in the fall. Then, something else occurred to him, a more recent conversation about…what was the name? It was not Thorne, he was quite certain of that.

"Well, what about you?" Jessica asked, looking at him over the candlelight. "You haven't said anything about the women in your life. I'm certain there have been several." Her dark eyes sparkled as she spoke teasingly, but Mark merely shrugged and grinned.

"I went steady for two months during my senior year in high school, and gave away my fraternity pin one summer while in college." He grinned. "That was the closest I've come to a permanent relationship."

"Sounds pretty uncomplicated," she said, wishing he would tell her more.

He frowned. "In a way it was. Occasionally I run into Gina, my college sweetheart, and wonder if I messed up. She's turned into a wonderful woman. She's married now and teaches kindergarten in Birmingham." He grinned at Jessica. "She married a friend of mine, in fact. But they seem to be well suited for one another."

Jessica listened, wondering if he was really hiding a broken heart. Every now and then, she was certain a shadow passed over his face as he looked over the evening crowd.

She wasn't so sure this guy didn't have a few secrets of his own, but she could not ask more without being rude.

The waitress appeared with a dessert menu but they waved it aside. Jessica shook her head, and Mark agreed.

"I couldn't possibly. It'll take a long walk on the beach tonight before I can ever settle down to bed."

As they drove home in silence, Jessica noticed that Mark seemed to be deep in thought. She wondered if it bothered him that she had been married. With some people it didn't matter, with some it did. What he didn't know was how quickly the romance had faded from the marriage. It was as though Blake became bored with her. He was like a little boy fascinated with a toy in a shop window; but once the toy belonged to him, he began looking around for something else to amuse him.

She closed her eyes for a moment, recalling the sarcasm that had begun to edge Blake's tone, and worse, the temper tantrums that she had been forced to endure in silence, for fear of provoking him further.

"Well, home again." Mark broke the silence as he steered his white Corvette into the driveway. When his headlights flashed over the two-story house, Jessica suddenly felt a wave of loneliness sweep over her. She considered inviting him in, and yet wasn't sure how she felt about that, so she said nothing.

He was getting out of the car, coming around to open her door. As she stepped out into the shadows, his hand cupped her elbow, guiding her gently along the path to the front porch.

"Thanks for dinner," she said as they reached the steps. "And for rescuing me from my morning disaster."

The reference to the coffee-stained blouse seemed to break the mounting tension between them.

He chuckled. "My pleasure."

Their eyes met and held for a moment before Jessica occupied herself with locating her door key.

"Here, let me," he said, taking the key from her hand and unlocking the door. The door swung open, and Mark frowned, looking into the dim hall. "You're not afraid here?"

"No, but I won't be alone after this week. A woman from Canada will be living here for awhile. Her name is Wilma Grayson and she'll be helping me with housekeeping."

"Good," he smiled. "I'm sure you'll need all the help you can get. Well, good night." He reached out, squeezing her hand.

"Good night," she smiled, gently releasing his hand.

As his steps receded down the walk, Jessica drew a deep breath and closed the door. It seemed ages since she had dated anyone, and she felt awkward about saying good night. Yet Mark had handled the situation well; as a matter of fact, he had handled the entire evening well. She wandered to the window, watching the taillights of his car disappear into the darkness.

He was a great guy. Yet, as she thought about him, she suspected he was not telling her everything about himself. Why not?

Four

Jessica's head rolled on the pillow as she struggled to interpret a nagging sound somewhere in the background. Her mind fought its way through a fog of sleep and slowly her eyes opened.

The telephone. It was the telephone on her bedside table.

She sat up on her elbow, frowning at her clock. 9:00 A.M. She blinked. Why was she still in bed? Then she remembered. Today was Sunday, her day to sleep in. And just who had the nerve to wake her on a Sunday?

She grabbed the phone and barked an irritated hello.

"Oops, sorry," a male voice said. "I know I'm rude to call this early."

She bolted upright, recognizing Mark's voice and suddenly not minding that he had awakened her.

She swallowed, trying to find her voice. "Mark? Hi. What's up?" She leaned back against the pillows as her eyes roamed to the window and met sun rays dancing on the window sill.

"Jessica, I wanted to ask a favor."

She frowned. A favor this early in the morning? "What is it?"

"Well...."

Jessica wiggled against the sheet, her curiosity mounting. "Go on, Mark," she laughed. "It must be important."

"It is. My sister, Felicia, and her family popped in late last night on their way to visit our folks. I've volunteered to babysit. Felicia and Bryan wanted a couple of hours at the beach before going on to Birmingham. I was wondering...."

Jessica waited, trying to anticipate this favor that he seemed so reluctant to ask.

"You're babysitting. How can I help?" she prompted.

She was feeling less enthused about this telephone call. Still, Mark Castleman had come to her rescue when she poured hot coffee all over herself. She owed him one. And she liked him.

"I'm going to take the twins out for a ride," he answered, "and I wondered if we could stop in to see you."

She smiled at that. "Sure."

"Thanks! We're about to make a drive through a breakfast place, so I'm taking orders."

She hesitated. "I'm not much for breakfast."

"Then I'll surprise you. Would thirty minutes from now be too soon to barge in?"

"That'll be fine," she said, although she wasn't so sure.

"Thanks, Jessica. You're terrific."

She smiled again. "See you soon."

She bounded out of bed and headed for the shower. If anyone else had asked her to help babysit twins at nine on a Sunday morning, she would have felt used. She didn't feel that way about Mark. In fact, she found herself looking forward to the day ahead.

Her shower and shampoo were taken care of in record time. Dressed in jeans and T-shirt, she hurried downstairs just as a maroon station wagon turned in to the driveway.

She spotted two small redheads in car seats in the back, and then she looked at Mark and began to laugh. He was getting out of the car, balancing two sacks in his arms with a bulging diaper bag dangling from his shoulder. Unlocking the door, she hurried across the porch and down the steps to meet him.

"I'd say you could use a little help," she called, relieving him of the two sacks.

He turned to her, looking a bit sheepish. His hair was slightly tousled, and the white golf shirt already held a fresh stain. He obviously hadn't had time to shave, but he was still handsome, and more endearing than ever in his vulnerable state.

"This is Molly and Mike," he called over his shoulder, opening the back door.

"And this must be your sister's car."

"That's right; no place for these seats in my Corvette."

Jessica looked in at two adorable round faces capped by thick red curls. "Hi, there. Want to come in and see me?" she called.

Molly began to coo and gurgle while Mike surveyed her with a look of suspicion.

"Tell you what," Mark glanced over his shoulder. "I can manage the twins if you can get the diaper bag."

Jessica shifted her load and extended a free arm as Mark hooked the diaper bag over her shoulder. He was so close to her she could smell a wonderful cologne, and the appreciative look in his green eyes brought a smile to her lips. "You do need help," she teased.

"That's what friends are for, right?"

She laughed. "I suppose. Why don't I go put my load down and hold the door open for you guys?"

"Good idea." His voice was muffled as he leaned into the backseat, unhooking seat belts.

Racing back to the porch, she began to giggle. What a funny situation he had gotten himself into, and yet she liked him even better as she thought about the good deed he was doing.

Breakfast smells drifted up from the white sacks as she hurried to the table. Ah, a free meal, and breakfast at that, which had become almost obsolete in her life.

By the time she returned to the door, he was already on the porch with a chubby little body in each arm.

She laughed at the sight of him bearing two little bundles of red hair and curious blue eyes. Pushing open the screen door, she touched a dimpled hand. "Hi there."

An excited sound greeted her as Mark trudged past, bearing his load.

"I don't have a high chair," she called, suddenly panicked about what to do with them.

"Neither do I," he responded, setting them both down in the middle of the kitchen floor.

"How old are they?" she asked, looking from one to the other. Each wore a blue sailor suit, a boy's and a girl's, accenting their beautiful blue eyes.

"Ten months. And not yet walking, which is why I thought their parents needed some rest for their aching backs."

Jessica smiled, kneeling down beside them. She reached out to Molly whose warm hand instantly clamped down on Jessica's finger.

"Mark, they're adorable! And they seem so good-natured."

"Just like their uncle," he chirped, digging through the diaper bag and coming up with a handful of toys. Depositing an assortment of toys before them, he straightened and pressed a hand to his back. "Good thing I'm in shape. They must each be a solid twenty pounds. Come on, let's eat."

Jessica frowned. "But —" Her eyes moved on to Mike, who had just latched onto his rubber duck and was chewing on its bill.

"They'll be fine for at least two minutes. Maybe we can wolf down a sausage and biscuit."

"What about them? Are they hungry?"

"They're overloaded with oatmeal and bananas. And I have backups in the bag."

Jessica laughed and stood up, still a bit anxious. "Thank goodness I mopped the floor yesterday."

"Don't worry about it," he touched her shoulder. "Sis assured me that dirt doesn't kill them."

Jessica shrugged, not so sure. On the other hand, she had never seen such healthy looking babies, so their parents must be doing all the right things.

Behind her, the sacks began to rattle as Mark withdrew containers of juice and neatly wrapped goodies until the table was full of food.

"If I had known you were bringing all this, I would have been calling you first."

"Hold on to that optimism. You may need it soon."

She arched an eyebrow. "Mark Castleman, are you hinting that I should change a dirty diaper?"

"Not yet," he winked. "I did that before we left home."

She laughed, dropping into a chair beside him while glancing back at the twins, happily entertained. "You are truly amazing. Your sister must really appreciate this."

"She'd better. I intend to collect the favor one of these days."

"How?" she asked, amused.

Mark grinned. "I'll think of something." He had opened the bottles of juice and unwrapped a sausage and biscuit for Jessica and himself. "Of course Felicia would remind me that I'm way in debt on favors." He took a huge bite, glancing down at the twins.

Jessica did the same, and as they chewed their food and watched Mike with his duck, and Molly with her pink rattle, a feeling of utter joy filled Jessica. Glancing back at Mark, she shook her head.

"You are full of surprises, Mr. Castleman."

He nodded, his cheeks bulging with food.

"Did you know you were having company?" she asked. "You didn't mention it last night."

"Nope. Felicia gives everyone an open invitation to visit her any time, and she expects the same. Five minutes after I got home, she telephoned to say they were only an hour away. That gave me enough time for an emergency cleanup."

Mike was bored and had begun to amuse himself by tossing his toys across the floor. Molly watched him, thoroughly entertained by her brother's antics.

"How long are they staying?" Jessica asked, fascinated with the twins.

"Leaving this afternoon. That's why I can be such a devoted uncle on short notice."

"Oh, I see," she smiled at him as she finished her breakfast.

"Here, have another one." He pushed another wrapped goody across to her.

She pressed her stomach. "I can't possibly."

"You must. Otherwise, big Mike will be crawling up on the table to eat a bite, then throw a bite. He alternates between the two."

Jessica dropped to her knees and sat down before the twins.

Mike had finished his game of throwing and was now frowning as he looked her over.

"I'm glad you two came to visit," she said.

Molly had dropped her toy and was extending her chubby arms to Jessica.

"Oh, you want to come see me?" Jessica called, pleased that Molly seemed to like her.

"Careful," Mark called, but it was too late.

When Jessica tried to lift her, she almost toppled forward before Mark's arms came around her waist, steadying her.

"I warned you. They're like two bowling balls!"

"No, they're not," Jessica scolded Mark, looking down into Molly's big blue eyes. "They're just healthy, aren't you darling?"

"Very healthy," Mark chuckled.

Mike had begun to yell his resentment at being left on the floor, and Mark was left to deal with him as Jessica walked around with Molly.

"Do you like my house?" she asked, hugging Molly

against her. She was a solid, warm bundle of joy, and Jessica thought she had never seen such a pleasant child. Absently, she touched a soft little curl, fascinated by its red sheen.

"Like her hair?" Mark called from behind her.

"It's beautiful." She glanced back at Mark. "Does red hair run in your family?"

He hesitated for a moment as he grabbed up empty wrappers and containers. "Apparently."

"Silly. Does Felicia have red hair?"

"Strawberry blonde," he said, finishing with the table and turning to Mike.

Jessica touched Molly's cheek. "You are adorable, yes you are."

"Adorable and sleepy, I think. Mike's eyelids are beginning to droop."

Jessica had strolled back to the kitchen and was peering down into Mike's grim little face. Mark was playing a game of airplane with him. When Mike rewarded him with a big smile, Mark grinned proudly. Watching this, Jessica suddenly felt her heart turn over. The nicest man she had ever met stood before her, caring for his sister's twins, who obviously adored him.

How did I get so lucky? Jessica thought, remembering how they had met on the beach, and again in the grocery store.

"Listen, I think I better take them back now," he said.

"Oh, must you?" Jessica was genuinely disappointed.

He hesitated, as his eyes moved from her to Molly and back again. "I don't want to go," he said softly. "Molly seems to like you as much as I do."

Mike let out a shriek, startling both of them. Jessica reached over, touching his warm little cheek. "Are you ready to go back to your parents?" she asked gently.

Crocodile tears were forming in his blue eyes, prompting Mark into action.

"Uh-oh. Time to ride." He hurried back to the kitchen, grabbing the diaper bag.

"Here, I'll get the toys," Jessica offered, trying to hurry although it was difficult with Molly filling her arms.

"Allow me," Mark said, extending another arm for Molly.

Jessica reluctantly gave her back, then helped by scooping up toys and placing them in the diaper bag.

Mike was already starting to sniffle as Mark charged toward the front door. "He likes to ride," he called back. "That's why I'm not wasting any time."

"Good idea," Jessica agreed, trailing after them.

In record time, Mark had them in their car seats, with more toys tucked around them. He closed the door, grabbed the diaper bag, then leaned down to give Jessica a peck on the cheek.

"You're wonderful," he said, smiling into her eyes.

"Thanks. So are you guys." She was careful to include all of them as Mark jumped in behind the wheel and cranked the engine.

She began to wave first at the twins in the back seat, then at Mark, as he backed the car out smoothly, turned and drove away.

Jessica stared after them, her arms folded, her mind filled with wonderful thoughts.

What a heartwarming experience it had been. She had seen another side to Mark, and she was dangerously close to liking him much more than she wanted to.

Why not like him? an inner voice whispered back.

She strolled toward the house, deep in thought. *Yes, why not?* She had been through a miserable time, but meeting Mark seemed to be the best thing that had happened to her. Maybe her life was poised for a pleasant change.

Five

❧

The painter was named Clarence and he was given to lengthy discussions of two topics — politics and the Scriptures. Since she and Clarence appeared to be on different sides of the political fence, Jessica chose to avoid that particular subject; but she soon began to feel just as uncomfortable about the Scriptures.

"Are you a Christian?" he demanded, when she handed him a mug of coffee before he began his work.

"Why…, yes, I am," she replied, startled. "Are you?"

"Been a Christian since I was fifteen. That's when I got dunked at Wiley's Lake, up in Dothan, after a revival at our church out at Miller Flats —"

"Clarence," she interrupted, glancing at her watch, "is there any problem about the paint? I mean, do you think you have enough?"

He was a small man with gray hair, thinning on top, but still thick around the brow line and above the ears. He had keen dark eyes and a sharp jaw line which he angled right to left when considering a question.

"Reckon I do," he answered, finishing his coffee.

"Well, just so you understand, I'm on a very tight budget and—"

"I won't waste a speck of paint, and I'll do the best job of anybody you could have hired. And I can finish that cupola up there for you." He frowned. "Why wasn't it finished before?"

She hesitated. Blake had liked the idea of the cupola, but the carpenter he met in a bar had been abysmally incompetent. On the second day, he had thrown up his hands and walked off the job. It had been just one more thing that Blake had started, then never got around to finishing. And even she had delayed tackling the project, hoping more money would be forthcoming. But of course that was not the case, and now she simply had to make the best of things.

Jessica had a good feeling about Clarence. With money scarce, she was down to instinct and guts in making a decision. She stood at the window, watching him thoughtfully.

He had gone out to haul the ladder from the back of his older model truck, which looked as though it had suffered the brunt of a misplaced ladder on the fender, and again on the back of the cab.

Jessica took a deep breath, fortifying herself with more tea as she thought about a Bible verse he had quoted. These days, she felt an occasional jab of guilt over not going to church. And she wasn't even sure where her Bible was packed. The truth was, she had become disillusioned about her faith, but maybe that, too, was about to change. It was amazing how much better she felt since meeting Mark Castleman. Her optimism was slowly returning, along with her faith in human beings, and perhaps even in the workings of God.

Mark sat in his office, his chair turned toward the glass wall that overlooked the city, the telephone receiver pressed against his ear. He had been talking to his mother about the painting he had mentioned to Jessica. This had prompted a few questions from his mother about the interesting woman he had just met. Mark had sidetracked her, saying she was just a friend. Then he had proceeded to talk about the bed and breakfast Jessica was planning to open in the Victorian house.

"I'm impressed," his mother said. "She must be quite a girl. Mark...," she hesitated.

"What is it?"

"Do you think you'll stay in Florida?"

He could hear the hurt that she tried to hide, and he was torn between guilt and honesty.

"I don't know, Mom. I have to do this. You know why."

A heavy sigh had filled the wire. "Yes, I do."

His parents had shown tremendous faith and courage when he told them about the plan that had nagged him for years. They had warned that he might be opening himself up to some disappointment and heartache, once he set out to find the man and woman who brought mixed emotions to all of them — gratitude and happiness, followed by fear and worry.

Still, Mark felt that he had to go on with his search. And Mark's father had finally admitted that if he were in Mark's shoes, he would probably be doing the same thing. There had been several tearful conversations with both his mom and dad, and they had assured him they would always love and support him, no matter what happened.

"Are you still there?" Her soft voice slipped into his thoughts and he straightened in his chair.

"I was just thinking about how wonderful you and Dad have been, and how much I appreciate you." He sighed. "There'll be a lot to talk about when I come home."

"I hope that will be soon," she said.

"Me too. Love you."

They finished their good-byes and he turned in his chair, replaced the phone and sat staring at his neat desk. His thoughts kept returning to Jessica. He couldn't seem to get her out of his mind.

Then the buzzer on the intercom sounded and he sat up even straighter in the chair and flipped the switch.

"He wants to see you," the efficient secretary announced.

"Thanks." Mark closed his eyes, while a flurry of conflicting emotions assaulted his brain, then slowly settled in place. When finally his head had cleared, he stood up, stretching his neck against his starched collar. He smoothed his paisley tie and walked to the door, mentally preparing himself for his morning meeting with Jack Barkley.

Maryanne, Barkley's administrative assistant for the past ten years, sat beside his desk, a stack of papers earmarked for their morning meeting. As usual, she wore a tailored business suit with just the right touch of gold jewelry.

"Here are the mortgages that are overdue," she spoke matter-of-factly, carefully laying the papers before him. "Two have already been given final notices and one is ready for foreclosure."

Jack adjusted his glasses, peering down at the papers. He tried to pull a full breath into his lungs, as the fresh air drifted in from his open window. From the corner of his eye, he noted that Maryanne was looking at the window curiously. She was a tactful person; that's why he liked her. She had not mentioned his recent habit of opening windows in February.

His hand dragged over the papers, as he picked them up, one by one, holding them close to his face. He hesitated over one name in particular. He frowned, staring into space, remembering a disturbing conversation with his chief attorney.

"We have to resolve this," Walt had complained. "You recall the incident I mentioned to you, the boating accident? The woman's attorney claims you were in your boat and sped right by, with her husband drowning before your eyes. I assured them the matter is preposterous; we'll take it to court if they're brave enough...."

Anger surged through Jack as he carelessly tossed the papers down and moved on. Nowadays, everyone had their hands outstretched, using trickery and treachery and outright lies to get his money.

His breath jerked through his lungs and for a moment, the room darkened. He blinked, staring straight ahead, fighting for control.

Just then the door opened. As Mark Castleman came into view, the expression on Jack's face began to change. His scowl disappeared, and he pushed the frames of his glasses higher on his nose.

"Come in, Mark," he said, smiling as the young man approached his desk.

J essica Thorne, you must have worked yourself to death!"
Wilma Grayson exclaimed.

She stood, hands on hips, regarding the mint-green walls of the small bedroom that she would occupy. Wilma wore her brown hair clipped close to her head on top, falling into deep waves on each side of her face. Her fair skin was wrinkled from many hours of fishing alongside her husband throughout the Canadian Rockies. They had traveled extensively during breaks from their teaching jobs. Since losing her husband, Wilma treasured each and every memory.

"I have worked hard, but I really didn't mind," Jessica said, raising her voice above the hammering overhead.

The smell of fresh paint drifted from the pantry, and Jessica walked over to close the door. She smiled at Wilma.

"If you aren't careful, you'll step in a paint bucket someplace."

"It's a nice smell," Wilma said. "I've always said homes deserve as much care as humans." She looked back at Jessica and smiled gently. "I expect you've had a rough time. Mrs.

Tillotson has told me something of your tragedy, so you needn't trouble yourself repeating it." She was regarding Jessica through faded blue eyes that had witnessed all sorts of human drama in her fifty-one years.

Jessica nodded, grateful to be spared. "The important thing now is to get this place in operation. My parents are sending some furniture this week. They're cleaning out their attic, and pressing family and friends for contributions as well." She paused, smiling. "I've abandoned my dream of antiques for now." Her brown eyes moved over the small guest room which held only a few simple pieces, but Wilma seemed delighted.

"You have that handsome buffet in the dining room," Wilma pointed out, "and the cherry bedroom suites, and some nice tables spaced about."

Jessica nodded. "As soon as I have the money, I'm going to make a trip up to the Smokies and bring back some wonderful handmade rockers and swings; and I'll pick up some accessories to add character to the house. By the way," she glanced back at Wilma, "I'll be moving out of the front bedroom. I plan to stay in the small room off the kitchen."

Wilma remembered the closet-sized room and frowned. "Don't you want me to take that one? I'm accustomed to small rooms."

Jessica shook her head. "No, I want you up here with the guests. That way you can be certain the other three bedrooms and baths stay fresh."

Wilma nodded, thinking that made sense too. "And the cooking? You want me to help with the cooking, don't you?"

Jessica hesitated. She didn't want to offend this pleasant woman, but she had some definite ideas about her meals.

"I've given a lot of thought to the food," she replied, temporarily sidetracking Wilma's questions. "I'm going all out for the breakfast, from homemade croissants and whole-wheat-pancakes to a special bacon that will be shipped down from a plant in Tennessee. And a dear friend in Angel Valley is sending honey from her own beehives. It's the best honey in the whole world. Dinner will be optional. Most B&B's don't offer dinner, but I plan to add the extras to this place."

"Sounds wonderful," Wilma beamed. "You'll have your own way of doing things, I'm sure, but I can set the table, wash the dishes, whatever. You just tell me how I can be a help and not a hindrance."

Jessica's brown eyes glowed as she looked at Wilma, certain now that she had a real treasure in this woman. She laced her fingers together and paced across the bedroom, her enthusiasm mounting. "I have a lot of plans, but I just have to pace myself, go slow and do it right."

Wilma was shaking her head. "I'm sure you'll do everything right, Jessica." Her eyes ran down the slim body of the young woman dressed in a long denim jumper over a white T-shirt. She wore no jewelry or makeup, yet Jessica Thorne conveyed an image of sophistication and class. Eyeing her thick dark hair and soft olive skin, Wilma thought she was one of the prettiest young women she had seen in a long time.

"So," Jessica turned back, "do you think this arrangement will suit you?"

Wilma laughed softly. "It's an answer to my prayers."

Jessica nodded, thinking it was time to get back to a few prayers of her own. And yet, when she tried to pray, she seemed to have a mental block.

"I've been very lonely," Wilma continued. "We reared three girls, but now they have their own lives. I don't want to interfere."

"I'm sure you wouldn't. Where do your daughters live?"

"Donna, the oldest, is married with two children and living in Vancouver. Robin is single and lives in a different place every year," she laughed softly. "She has a degree in education, but she hasn't found her niche yet, or so she tells me. Amy, the youngest, just married last Christmas. She and her husband are teachers in Cranbrook."

Jessica studied the woman as she spoke of her children, seeing the pride in her eyes. "Sounds like you have a nice family."

Wilma nodded. "Each girl was very different from the others, but that made for some interesting times!"

"Yes, I suppose so."

Jessica became aware of a persistent knocking below. She excused herself and hurried down the stairs. The postman stood at the door, a registered letter in his hand.

She opened the door and greeted the postman with a smile. "Good morning."

"Morning!" His head was turned to the side, as he focused his attention on the end of the house. "Pink? You're painting the outside pink?"

Jessica remembered a patch of paint she had tried on a board as an experiment.

"Pale pink," she replied confidently. "I bet you'll like it once we're finished."

He scratched his head, avoiding a reply as he extended the official-looking letter. "You'll have to sign for this."

Jessica reached for the pencil and jotted her name on his

pad, then focused on the crisp white envelope in her hand. *Mrs. Blake Vandercamp* was neatly typed, along with the address, just to the right of the stamp of certification. This looked very official. Then her eyes widened on the return address and she held her breath. The Barkley Corporation!

She mumbled her thanks to the postman, then closed the door. Her feet flew over the polished board floors as she sought the privacy of the study. Closing the door behind her, she rushed to the desk and sat down, ripping the envelope with her thumbnail.

A brief and formal notice informed her that she was now two months past due with her mortgage payment, in addition to the late charges which had been tallied up for the past months.

She gasped, unable to believe what she was seeing. The late charges went back several months before she had married Blake. How could that be? Hadn't Blake noticed what he was signing? Surely he had not been late with his payments every month. The crisp white paper slipped from her trembling fingers as she yanked open the bottom drawer and removed the expanding file of checks, neatly compartmentalized by month. She dug into each month, locating the mortgage checks, inspecting the date on each one.

Blake had told her the payments were due on the fifteenth of the month, and she had been precise in doing that, aware of late fees. Somehow she and Blake together had managed to accumulate over five hundred dollars in late fees, and now she had to pay the two thousand dollars monthly mortgage or…

She pounced on the paper again, staring at the legal jargon and correctly interpreting its meaning. If the late fees and the mortgage were not settled within the next month, the owner could foreclose, as outlined in the contract.

Outlined in the contract?

She opened and closed drawers in a frantic search. What had she done with the contract? It was not in the files where she kept those papers; had it ever been? Was it possible Blake had taken it out before the accident?

Her heart was thudding in her throat, and she suddenly felt as though all the blood in her body were rushing to the top of her head. She wondered if she was about to have a stroke.

She swallowed hard, pressing icy hands against her temples, trying to calm her nerves. This was ridiculous; she was having an anxiety attack. One did not lose a home over being a little late with the month's mortgage or carelessly allowing late charges to accrue.

Tossing her head back, she stared at the ceiling and took several slow, deep breaths. She would find the contract; she would prove to herself that there was no need to panic.

Slowly, the confusion in her brain began to settle. *The contract! You've seen it somewhere. Where is it?* She searched her mind for answers.

Then it came to her. The lockbox, of course, with a copy of the death certificate, the insurance papers, and other important documents. She returned to the desk, withdrawing the tiny key from the middle drawer. Opening another drawer, she removed the small metal box. Fitting the key in the lock with fingers that worked at being steady, she managed to get the box open. There, right on top, was the document.

Unfolding the paper, her eyes scanned each line until she

came to an abrupt halt on the crucial words which Blake had so carelessly signed. She sank back in the chair, sick at heart. Barkley's legal sharks had, in fact, drawn up an agreement that could take the house away from her unless she came up with twenty-five hundred dollars in a hurry. And this was the first official notification she had received. Or was it? She pressed her hand to her forehead, trying to think. No, there had been others, but she always knew she would pay every month, even if she ran a few days late. She had never heard of this; there had to be some recourse.

She recalled how she had been forced to pay off Blake's charge cards and settle past-due accounts at half a dozen department stores in order to obtain local credit. Thank goodness, her past credit record was excellent, and this was the main reason she had decided to take back her maiden name. Still, merchants and bankers here knew her husband was Blake Vandercamp. They seemed to be watching her with guarded optimism, wondering if she would be as irresponsible as her husband had been. For that reason, in juggling her monthly bills, she had paid the wrong people first. Or so it now seemed.

The walls seemed to close in on her as her mind raced to find a solution. She hadn't the heart to tell Blake's parents that he had cashed out the life insurance policy they had so lovingly paid on all those years. Nor could she ask her parents for more money. They had drained half their savings to help her redo the house.

Foolishly, she had used half the money allotted for the monthly mortgage payment to finish the outside of the house. She had planned to stall on her monthly payment for a couple more weeks. By that time, the loan she had applied for at the bank would come through. Or would it?

Blake's parents! There was no other way now. She'd simply have to go to them, tell them everything. The thousand dollars they had given her to help on the house had been a gift of love, in their minds. This was the other reason she had not told them about Blake's indebtedness. She had put that money on the bill at the funeral home, using the last of her savings as well.

She placed her elbows on the desk, burying her throbbing head in her hands. Barkley; it always came back to him. And of course if she went to her father-in-law with the financial situation, he would start screaming lawsuit again.

She turned tearful eyes to the crisp white letterhead bearing the Barkley insignia. All the peace and hope of the morning had been obliterated by the man who was becoming a monster in her mind. Mel was right! Barkley could have saved Blake's life if he had stopped the boat. And now, he dared to threaten her. No, it wasn't simply a threat. He was going to take away the only source of income she would have, the one ray of hope in her life. This house that she loved and tended like a firstborn.

She leapt to her feet, pacing the room. No! He was not going to do that. Maybe he had forced her into a corner, but this time she was going to come out fighting. Yes, she would fight him with everything she had. And in the process, she would scream to the newspapers, television, the entire world what a ruthless, insensitive human being he really was.

Seven

J essica had set an appointment with her attorney for the following Monday morning. She had hoped to see him right away, but he had informed her he was tied up in court the remainder of the week. In her most businesslike tone of voice, she had apprised him of the situation with Barkley. He had advised her to do nothing until they could review her options together. The tone of defeat that usually edged his voice at the mention of Barkley began to change as she expressed her determination to file a lawsuit. She would even bring in the media, if necessary, to tell her story about that day he had ignored her cries for help.

"I'll clear my calendar for Monday morning," he assured her. "In the meantime, say nothing to anyone about this."

She tried to draw hope from that conversation as she worked through the week. She kept Clarence fortified with iced tea, and he kept her in Scripture. She was getting accustomed to his biblical philosophies; furthermore, she no longer minded. He had completed the cupola, and she was stunned by how perfectly it fit the house. Also, he was working a miracle on the old board siding, bringing out of its gray shadows the glistening pink, Victorian dream that had warmed her heart.

Working twelve hours a day helped keep at bay Barkley's threat, while she occupied her mind with the house. Anxiously, she watched and waited for a delivery truck to arrive with the furniture her parents were sending.

On Thursday, an express truck drove up. At the sight of the truck, she bolted out of the house to meet the driver. He was delivering a large cardboard box, bearing a return address in Birmingham.

Eagerly, she cut through the protective cardboard and gently removed the carefully wrapped painting, gasping as she did so.

"Wilma," she called over her shoulder, eager to share her joy with her new employee. "Come look."

Wilma hurried down the stairs with her broom and dustpan, a smudge of dirt on her nose. Jessica smiled at the smudge, feeling true affection for Wilma. The woman had quickly won Jessica's heart with her pleasant attitude and her willingness to pitch in wherever needed. A deep friendship was developing.

"That's lovely!" Wilma gasped.

Jessica stared at the lovely painting of two little girls on the beach, surrounded by soft pastels. She shook her head in awe.

"Mark was right. This is absolutely perfect for the house. Will you help me hang it?" She smiled at Wilma, who was nodding and regarding the picture wide-eyed.

"Of course. And it *is* perfect."

That evening, seated at her desk in the study, Jessica thumbed through the telephone directory, searching for Mark's number. There was no listing for him. Her short nails drummed impatiently on the freshly polished mahogany desk.

Since he was new to the area, his name had not been included in the directory. She lifted the receiver and dialed information. After inquiring about a Mark Castleman, she was given the phone number. She punched in the numbers, nervously twirling the phone cord between her thumb and forefinger. He was probably out for the evening, she told herself, perhaps having dinner with some pretty woman he had just met.

"Hello."

The sound of his voice brought to Jessica's mind the memory of his warm smile, and she suddenly felt the week's oppression drain away.

"Mark!" she spoke lightly, "Hi, this is Jessica."

"Jessica! What's going on at the beach?"

"Rain at the moment. Did your sister and her family have a good visit with you?"

"The twins cried after me when they had to leave. I guess that means they like me."

"Can't blame them," she said with a smile.

"Thanks again for helping out. It was the best possible way for me to kill an hour. I really appreciate it."

"It was my pleasure. Listen, Mark, I called to tell you the painting arrived, and it's really pretty. You have no idea how wonderful it looks on the wall upstairs." She hesitated, carefully choosing her words. "I'll merely consider it a loan; otherwise, I couldn't possibly keep it."

"Why not? Mom has redecorated and now the painting is just taking up space in a closet. I'm glad it suits your house."

Jessica smiled at his kindness, then voiced the other reason she had phoned.

"I was wondering if you could come out for dinner on Saturday evening."

"Well…sure. I've heard about a new seafood house opening up over on Thomas Drive and — "

"What I had in mind," she interrupted gently, "was cooking for you here at the house." She laughed nervously. "I need to start experimenting with some of my recipes before tourist season begins." It was the truth, and yet she knew she would prepare something really special for him. She hoped he didn't think she merely wanted to use him for a guinea pig.

He chuckled good naturedly. "Okay. I'm game for almost anything. Believe me, I'm sick of fast foods and frozen dinners. I don't know how I manage to mess up a microwave dinner, but I can do it."

Jessica laughed, remembering a few of her own disasters. "I'm glad you're free for Saturday. Is six o' clock okay?"

"Fine. I'll look forward to it."

She hung up and stared into space, a smile drifting over her small features. She took a deep breath. Maybe for just a few hours, she could forget about Barkley!

The rain continued throughout the week, adding to Jessica's frustration. The furniture still had not arrived. An anxious call to her mother confirmed her suspicions — the furniture had not left Louisville. Her mother apologized, detailing her bout with influenza.

"It's okay, Mother," Jessica interrupted smoothly, "but can you please get the furniture sent tomorrow?"

Her mother promised, apologizing again.

After Jessica hung up, she dropped her head in her hands, trying not to think about the two deadlines she was facing — the opening of her bed and breakfast by tourist season, and the overdue mortgage payments.

Jessica was humming to herself as she removed the bowl of spinach salad from the refrigerator and placed it on the counter. Then she reached back for the special vinaigrette dressing she had just prepared. The pleasant aroma of her casserole drifted over the kitchen as she checked the wall clock and reached for a gloved potholder. She had fifteen minutes before Mark was due to arrive.

She was pleased with the samples of food she had tasted, along with her preparation time. When she prepared for guests, she would follow the same routine, doubling all the ingredients.

Placing the baking dish on the counter, she peered at the fresh grouper, dusted with paprika, and surrounded with pilaf and fresh vegetables. The last minute addition of chopped bananas and walnuts was the finishing touch. She had managed to pry this recipe from a chef from Key West. She had met him and his wife at the seafood market she frequented. Overhearing his conversation with the market owner, she had boldly questioned him about his menus, which led to a cup of coffee and a friendly chat. The chef's wife had been interested in her bed and breakfast and had pressed her husband to share a good recipe for fresh fish.

Her eyes moved on to the basket of homemade rolls, resting beneath the white linen napkin. Her third attempt at baking bread had finally paid off. The crusty rolls oozed with a yeasty aroma that begged for a light drizzle of butter and an open mouth.

The doorbell rang and she jumped, almost dropping the basket of rolls on her way to the dining room table. Tightening her grip, she placed the bread beside the casserole and removed her gloved potholder. As she passed the hall mirror, she assessed her reflection while untying the strings of her chef's apron.

Her yellow silk blouse and matching slacks flared loosely about her slim figure, and the gold hooped earrings accented her dark hair and eyes. Her cheeks were flushed, but that was to be expected after an hour in the kitchen.

She opened the door to face Mark, and to her surprise, a nervous jolt hit her stomach at the sight of him. He was wearing olive green slacks and a beige linen shirt and holding a bouquet of red roses.

"Hi!" His eyes moved upward toward the roof of the porch. "I noticed the cupola when I got out of the car. It looks great. Your carpenter obviously knows his stuff."

"Clarence has proven to be a godsend," she smiled.

Mark extended the bouquet of roses. "For you," he grinned.

"Why, thank you, Mark. That was very thoughtful." She lifted the red velvet petals and sniffed gingerly. "You had no way of knowing, but roses are my favorite flower."

"Well," he shrugged, "most women favor roses." He bit his lip, wondering if he sounded like a real Casanova. "At least, that's what Mom always tells me. She has a magic touch with roses, keeps a beautiful garden."

"And do you help with the garden?" Jessica asked, opening the door for him.

"Not much," he admitted, shrugging. "I've never had a green thumb, just one that always finds the thorns."

"You found me," she said lightly, and he began to chuckle.

"Well, you're about the prettiest thorn I've ever encountered," he said as he stepped inside and began to sniff the air. "If the food tastes as good as it smells, your guests are going to be beating down the door every week."

Jessica laughed, leading the way back to the dining room. "You had better reserve your judgment until you've had a few bites. You just might change your mind."

"I doubt it," he said, as his eyes moved over the dining room.

The large table was set with a lace cloth, rose-patterned china and crystal goblets that Jessica had purchased at an outlet in Pigeon Forge.

"Want to light the candles?" she called over her shoulder, as she went into the kitchen to locate a vase.

"With pleasure," he said, picking up the book of matches on the buffet.

Jessica carefully arranged the roses in water, impressed again by Mark's thoughtfulness. She was actually grateful that she had bumped his cart and ruined the blouse; it had been a small price to pay for meeting such an extraordinary person. Suddenly, she remembered the painting and was anxious to show him how well it complemented the upper hallway.

Holding the vase, she returned to the dining room. The candles were lit, casting a romantic aura over the lovely table. When she added the roses as a centerpiece, she turned glowing brown eyes to Mark.

"Would you mind bringing roses every week? They're a perfect match for the china."

He nodded, admiring the tiny roses etched on the china plates. "They are, aren't they?"

"Come on, I want to show you something."

He looked puzzled, although he followed good-naturedly as she dashed up the stairs and stopped before the painting that graced the wall. As soon as his eyes found the painting, he began to nod.

"Yep, it's perfect there. Mom will be pleased."

"I'd like to call her, or at least drop her a note of thanks. I want to offer your parents two or three weekends here in return for the painting. Or if they want it back later on —"

"I think Mom has already filled up all the wall spaces at home. She'll be glad to know it suits your hall. Remind me to leave the number, or the address, before I go."

"I will," Jessica answered, turning back down the stairs. "I'd better keep an eye on dinner."

Mark folded his hands behind him and followed her back down to the kitchen, glancing around. He saw that she had managed to make the rambling kitchen a cozy spot as his eyes moved over the potted plants and assortment of baskets adorning the wall. He wondered if she had done the decorating herself, or if she had hired someone. She had told him she was working on a budget so this must be her own personal touch, and it was a nice one. She was quite a lady, he decided, as his eyes swung to the food, neatly displayed.

"Is there something I can do to help?" he asked.

She glanced back over her shoulder, unaccustomed to a

male offer of help. Her father rarely came near the stove, and Blake had never lifted a hand to help her. Might as well start off right with Mark Castleman, she decided.

"Yes. You can grab the ice bucket from the kitchen counter while I get the pitcher of tea. By the way, how are the twins?"

"Glad to be at Granny's house!"

Jessica laughed, watching Mark as he went to work in the kitchen as though he were an old hand at it, while she returned for lemon and orange slices. After they took their seats at the table and began to eat, neither spoke for several moments. Then Mark touched the napkin to his mouth and looked down the table to Jessica.

"Jessica, your food is fantastic. What kind of fish is this?"

"Grouper." She studied the oblong serving dish. "If you'll notice, I could feed a couple more people with this amount."

"At least," he grinned. "And I'm a big eater. I think you have your economics down when it comes to running a business."

At the mention of economics, Jessica lost her appetite. "I certainly hope so. I'm running this place on a shoestring."

"Oh?" His eyes were curious though he refrained from further questions.

Jessica sighed. "I'm afraid my husband was not very good at managing money. I've really gone in debt here, but I believe in the long run Seascape will pay for itself."

Mark studied her for a moment. "You'll make a go of it; I'm confident you will." His words were intended to encourage her, but he noticed that her expression remained grim.

"I have to succeed here," she replied quietly, thinking of Barkley. She looked from her food to the lovely roses, which reminded her of this wonderful man seated at her table. "Mark, you said you were raised in Birmingham," she said, trying to keep the conversation going. "I've never been there. Dad has, of course, and he went to a few Alabama football games. The Crimson Tide," she smiled at Mark. "That's my dad's favorite football team, even though we lived in the shadow of Big Orange!"

Mark chuckled. "Tennessee has a good team too, but yes — the Tide has a certain tradition about it, going back to Bear Bryant. The main campus is located in Tuscaloosa. It's a nice town with a warm friendly atmosphere. I thought about going to law school there, but I decided to stay in Birmingham." He looked at her. "Bet you made lots of friends in college."

She nodded. "I guess so. It was a funny thing; my roommate and I wore the same size clothing, right down to the shoes. We had fun swapping clothes." She paused for a moment, thinking about Charlotte. "We even swapped boyfriends once," she added, laughing.

"Swapped dates? You actually did that?" he teased. He was thinking she seemed far too sensible to be pulling pranks.

Jessica shook her head, thinking what a silly joke it had been. Those carefree days seemed long ago, for so much had happened since then. She certainly felt as though she had aged a decade, when in reality only a few years had passed since her college days.

"Swapped boyfriends," he repeated, shaking his head. "You don't seem the type to do that."

"It was a joke," she said, without elaborating. "Hey, I'm trying out a new dessert tonight. It's called raspberry lime pie. Ready to sample it?"

Mark hesitated. He didn't care much for limes, but he decided to be a good sport. "Okay, but first let me help you clear the table."

When they sat back down to dessert, Mark was pleasantly surprised after the first bite. "This is great, and I'm not much on lime. You've managed to blend everything together just right. And it's pretty," he said, noticing the color and texture.

Jessica couldn't conceal her surprise at his observations. He was so different from anyone she had ever known. She liked him more each time she was with him, and he was looking at her as though he felt the same way about her.

She dropped her eyes to her dessert, wondering suddenly if she hadn't better start guarding her feelings. For years, she had wished on stars for a man like Mark Castleman, but then Blake had come along and swept her off her feet before she ever got to know the man behind the charming smile. She couldn't bear to let herself be deceived a second time. In spite of appearances, she had better hold back with Mark. He was still a stranger, after all.

"When we finish the dishes, I suggest a walk on the beach," Mark was saying.

"The dishes?" she repeated, unable to mask her surprise this time.

"Sure! Unless you'd rather not have me touching these pretty plates."

"No, I don't mind that," she laughed, handing him an empty plate.

He was standing beside her, looking down into her face, and for a moment their eyes locked. Neither moved. He drew a deep breath, turning his attention toward the kitchen door. *Better watch your step, Castleman*, he silently admonished.

This lady could be gone with your heart before you ever miss it.

Deliberately, he turned the conversation to chitchat — beach news, weather, tides, tourists. When finally they had cleaned up the kitchen and returned to the front porch, he had managed to push aside his wariness about losing his heart. He really enjoyed being with her, so why not just see where it led?

Eight

❧

Jessica had slipped out of her sandals into her tennis shoes, ready for a stroll on the beach. As they stood on the back walkway, glancing around them, Mark tilted his head back, looking up at a full moon.

"We couldn't have picked a more beautiful night," he said, his hands in his pockets, his profile a silhouette in the moonlight.

"I know." Jessica dragged her eyes from his face and stared down at the beach.

The moon was spinning a silver mist over the ocean and the beach. While her house sat in a shelter of palms in the darkest area of beach, there was plenty of light from the moon for an evening stroll.

"Well, what are we waiting for?" Mark grinned down at her and reached for her hand.

Shyly, she slipped her hand in his as he opened the gate and they picked their way down the path to the beach. Jessica breathed deeply of the fresh sea mist and revelled in the beauty around her.

As they walked along, Mark glanced at her, noting the thoughtful look on her lovely features. He wondered exactly what she was thinking. Was she missing her late husband? Automatically, his large hand gripped her fingers a bit tighter. She must be having a rough time. What a terrible tragedy for both of them. He struggled to choose another topic, something safe and comfortable.

"Your dinner was fantastic," he said, as they followed the path near the edge of the ocean, a walking trail firmly packed down by the tide, yet not wet at the moment. "If the meal I had tonight was a sample of what your guests will be getting, you won't need to worry about a shortage of business. Where did you buy the grouper we ate tonight?"

"There's a great little seafood market about a mile from here," she answered. "The market always has good fish, and they're reasonably priced."

He nodded. "And what about the pie? Did you think up that recipe yourself?"

She laughed softly, relieved to be discussing pleasant things; simple things, like recipes. It was so nice to be with Mark Castleman who seemed to represent all the good and wholesome aspects of life. She didn't know him that well, and yet she felt sure of her judgment this time. She pushed her thoughts back to the subject of her special dessert.

"Interestingly enough, I got that recipe from Wilma, my friend from Canada. She's gone to visit a friend tonight; perhaps the next time you come, you can meet Wilma. She's a great lady."

They were approaching the condos that towered above the beach, half a mile from Seascape. Tiny squares of lights from hundreds of windows offset the glow of the moon, and the sound of voices from patios rose above the sounds of the ocean and their footsteps on the sand.

"I see quite a few people farther down," Mark said. "On a night like this, lots of people will be out for a stroll beneath a full moon. Want to keep going? Or are you ready to turn back?"

The weariness of the day, and the week as well, was taking its toll on Jessica. She stopped walking and glanced up at Mark. "I'm ready to head back if that's okay with you. Maybe I'll make us some cappuccino and we can sit on the porch for a while."

"Sounds great!"

Glancing back over her shoulder, Jessica remembered something she had been wanting to ask. "How far down is your condo?"

"Another mile or so." He named the condominium complex and Jessica nodded.

"That's a nice place."

Mark nodded too, gripping her hand tighter as they approached a rough spot in the sand. "Hey, I just thought of something. I have business that will keep me in Panama City until late tomorrow night." He hesitated, feeling a need to explain further. "I'm meeting with a man who is…who may be important in my future. I'll tell you more about it later. But what I wanted to ask you is this — how about attending the Seaside Chapel with me Sunday morning?"

Jessica caught her breath. She hadn't set foot inside a church since her wedding and didn't feel inclined to do so now. And yet Mark was a nice guy and it was hard to say no. Then she remembered Wilma.

"I'm sorry, but I can't. Remember the lady I told you

about who will be helping me with the housework? I've already promised to go out to lunch with her on Sunday and on to the mall. She wants to take me to a home accessories shop."

"Maybe another day," he offered casually.

She nodded, yet she refused to commit herself. There were many places she'd like to go with Mark, but right now church was not one of those places.

"How long did you say you'll be living here?" she asked, trying to find a different subject.

He hesitated. "My parents would like me to return to Birmingham," he said, willing to go that far with his thoughts. "But...I have some thinking to do."

His serious manner caught Jessica's attention. She glanced up at him. A deep frown marred his smooth brow as the moonlight slanted over his features. He had mentioned something about a former girlfriend marrying his best friend. That must be what he was trying to sort out in his mind. Thinking about how he must have felt in that circumstance, she felt a twinge of sympathy for him. That was one problem that had never faced her, and yet she would have preferred that dilemma to her own.

No, she inwardly scolded; she hadn't been given the option of choosing her punishment. She merely had been given an opportunity to learn from adversity and press on. This was the sentence her mother had given her many times over the past months. Amazing how valuable a mother's advice could be, she thought, realizing how that particular theme of learning from adversity kept popping up in her head these days.

Suddenly, a couple of joggers dashed past them, a boy

and girl who looked to be in high school. They were laughing and teasing one another, and Jessica almost envied the carefree abandon that seemed to surround them.

Mark had fallen silent, and now she was at a loss for words as well. She had never been one for chitchat, although it now seemed a necessary skill with tourist season fast approaching.

They were back at her gate, scraping the soles of their shoes.

"Maybe we walked off a few calories," she said with a grin.

His eyes swept her trim figure. "Calories don't seem to affect you at all."

She shrugged, walking ahead of him. "Weight hasn't been a problem so far, but my luck may run out one of these days."

"I doubt it," Mark said, settling into a rocker on the porch while she hurried inside to make the cappuccino. In the process, she switched on her old stereo, a relic from high school days, which still had a nice sound, particularly with a Kenny G instrumental. The soft music floated through the living room window to the porch, and as she took out the cups of coffee to join Mark, she heard him humming along softly.

Handing him the cup, she took a seat in the opposite rocker and drew a deep breath.

"Thanks," he said, sipping the flavored coffee as he leaned back in the rocker. "I could get really spoiled by this. Maybe I should leave a tip or something," he joked. "Otherwise, I could become a pest."

"Your tip is hanging on the upstairs wall," she laughed.

"However, I could place a deep dish on the hall table, and you could throw dollars at it on future trips." She laughed again, surprised at how easily laughter and jokes came up with Mark. He was bringing out a carefree side of her that she thought she had buried with Blake.

"Sounds like a fair bargain. I'll pass that along on the sly to your other guests, while they're making themselves comfortable out here on the porch."

"Sure! Pass the hat if you feel so inclined."

"Or the seashell. I noticed you have one in there about the size of a boot. I imagine we could cram quite a few dollars in that seashell."

"Oh, good idea. And while you're passing word along on the sly, tell everyone I prefer tens to ones."

"Right. Unless the ones are hundreds."

"Exactly."

She was laughing harder and she wondered if this was really as funny as it seemed, or if some of her tension was being drained through laughter. She was beginning to feel as though she had been poring over the college textbooks too long, cramming for a final, and now anything and everything could evoke the slightest giggle.

"This really is a beautiful spot," he said, looking around.

Jessica nodded thoughtfully. "I have big dreams for the house." She tried to suppress a deep sigh as the enormity of her undertaking swept over her. That was happening more often these days as the dark cloud of the mortgage seemed always to hover just above her head, even at good times, like now.

"Seems to me you're making those dreams come true. How long had you been wanting to run a B&B?" he asked, thinking it was a smart idea, and this certainly seemed like the perfect setting.

"I really had never given any thought to a bed and breakfast," she replied simply.

"Then how —" Mark cut off the question, thinking he was on the verge of prying again, but he wanted to know everything about her. He was fascinated that some twist of fate had put them on the same path that day; he was beginning to feel grateful and blessed for having met her.

"My husband was an entrepreneur," she replied slowly. "He was always looking for ways to make money. He thought this place was a real steal. As it turned out, the thievery was on the other end."

Mark stared at her, feeling that this time he had to ask. "Care to explain what you mean? Or is that too personal?"

She hesitated, staring out at the dark ocean. "Let's just say that my husband was taken in by a shrewd man whose attorneys have a special skill with the fine print in a contract."

Mark sat up straighter. "May I ask who sold you this place?"

She took a deep breath and spoke the name around tight lips. "A man by the name of Jack Barkley. I understand he's the most powerful man in Panama City." She looked across at him. "Be sure you steer clear of him. He's horrible."

Mark froze, staring at her, unable to believe what she was saying. Of course he had heard about some of Barkley's dealings, and he could see that the man was capable of such shrewdness. And yet....

He turned to stare out at the ocean, trying to collect his thoughts. How should he respond to that? Should he go on and admit his association with him? As he pondered the situation, Jessica stirred in the chair beside him.

"Sorry, I don't want to ruin our evening with the animosity I feel toward that man."

Mark swallowed, trying to muster up the right words. "Well, actually, I do know who Barkley is. But —" he hesitated, trying to lead into the subject.

"Please," she put up her hand, "could we change the subject? I have very strong feelings about the man, Mark. I can quickly ruin our evening once I get on the subject of that crook."

The moonlight was slanting down over her features, and yet even in the semidarkness, he could see the set of her chin, the firmness of her lips, and he saw, too, how the dark eyes seemed midnight black — and filled with contempt.

He couldn't believe his rotten situation. At last he had met a woman he could really care for, and already their relationship was doomed. Or it would be if he opened his mouth and revealed what he had been on the verge of telling her. His instincts told him to hold back, this was not the time to explain the situation. And if he did, she'd never see him again. He didn't want that to happen so he searched his mind for another topic of conversation.

"Are your folks coming down any time soon?" he asked.

"Maybe in a month or so. Dad can't get away until then."

He nodded, pretending to listen, but he kept thinking about the decision he must make. He glanced at his watch, remembering he had promised to make a phone call before midnight tonight. A call to Jack Barkley. He felt guilty just thinking about it, after what she had said. He had to get out of the chair and away from this beautiful woman.

From the corner of her eye, Jessica caught him checking

his watch. She felt embarrassed as she reflected on their evening together. She had probably bored him to death, centering the conversation on herself and her problems at Seascape. There had been so many things she had planned to ask him. How had she gotten so far off track?

"Listen, I really hate to leave good company," he was saying, "but I have some phone calls to make tonight."

Jessica wondered if she should offer the use of her phone, but of course he knew she had a telephone and wouldn't mind asking to use it. Obviously, the phone calls he wanted to make were private, or at least this was a polite excuse to leave.

She stood up, taking the cup from his hand.

"Well, thanks for bragging about my food," she smiled up at him. "You've boosted my confidence."

"I was just telling the truth," he said, staring down into her eyes.

Mark had been asking himself just how far he should push this relationship. After the startling announcement she had just made about Barkley, he had no idea what would happen. He shoved his hands in his pockets and tore his eyes from hers.

"Thanks for a wonderful evening," she spoke lightly, looking into his eyes.

He looked back into her face, and without thinking he leaned down and kissed her lips.

She was balancing two cups, which made for a quick kiss. Mark backed away then, knowing he was facing a problem with her, one that would require some thought before he saw her again.

"Well, good night, Jessica." He smiled into her eyes.

"Good night." Her voice was feather soft, as she watched the smile fade from his face, replaced by a look of serious concern.

What is he thinking? Jessica suddenly felt a stab of alarm as she realized how close she was to losing that tight grip she kept on her emotions.

As he walked away, Jessica stared after him, unable to move while he disappeared into the silvery night. As she turned back to the door she became aware that her heart was racing. She tried to calm her thoughts and push her mind toward a book to read in bed. She sauntered to the kitchen, placing the cups on the sink.

Then, slowly, she lifted a finger to touch her lips as she stared into space, already thinking about Mark Castleman again.

Nine

On Monday morning, Jessica parked her car before the tall
office building and hopped out. Smoothing the skirt of
her black linen dress, she hurried through the front door
of the building and paused in the lobby, scanning the directory for the office number of her attorney's firm.

As she walked to the elevator, she checked her watch,
annoyed to see that she was already five minutes late. She
had skipped breakfast in order to arrive on time, but then
Clarence had detained her in the drive, eager for conversation. She was trying to break away when Wilma, bless her,
came to the rescue, calling Clarence to the kitchen for a cup
of coffee.

The elevator door swung open and Jessica stepped on. As
the crowd closed in around her and the air grew thin, she
fought a mild attack of claustrophobia. She dropped her eyes
to her black patent pumps as the elevator glided to a halt at
the second floor, then the third. She took a deep breath,
looking impatiently at the door, as it slid open on the fourth
floor.

Stepping quickly from the elevator, she located Martin McCormick's office in the corner suite. Only a few people waited as Jessica walked through the plush lobby and gave her name to the receptionist. She took her seat and had just picked up a magazine when her name was called, and soon she was being ushered down a carpeted corridor to a huge office.

Across the room, behind a handsome cherry desk, Martin McCormick was talking on the telephone in a low voice. As she entered the room, he lifted a hand, waving her to a chair opposite his desk. She sat down and waited as he attempted to wind up his phone conversation. He was a small, well-groomed man with silver hair and ordinary features. He would not stand out in a crowd, or even a small gathering, but Jessica had heard he was quite impressive in a court-room.

Hanging up, he stood and extended his hand. "Sorry for the delay." He smiled briefly, then took his seat and surveyed her carefully.

"That's okay," she said, relieved that her tardiness hadn't caused any problem. "It's nice to finally meet you." Until now, their conversations had taken place over the telephone. She had begun to think that he wasn't taking her seriously until last week when she had angrily stated her intentions to sue Jack Barkley.

"I have some questions to ask you," he said, leaning forward in the chair and reaching for a silver pen.

They began to talk, and she detailed the story to him, watching the swift movements of his hand as the pen flew over the lines of a legal pad.

Again, she told him the story, noticing as she spoke that a

deep frown kept rumpling his forehead. At one point, he even put down the pen and stared at her, and she couldn't help wondering exactly what he was thinking. Still, he made no comment until she had finished the sordid tale, emphasizing how Barkley's boat had sped past while she screamed for help. And now...the final insult...his threat to evict her from her home.

Opening her purse, she withdrew the mortgage papers that Blake had so carelessly signed. "I brought these," she said, handing the papers to Martin McCormick.

He scanned the contents quickly, then breathed a heavy sigh. For several seconds he said nothing; he merely stared at his desk. Then, suddenly, as though remembering she was in the room, he punched a button. An efficient blonde swept into the room.

"Could you please make a copy of this?" he handed her the papers and she hurried out. "You'll want to keep the original." He smiled at Jessica.

Jessica watched him carefully. He said nothing as he stared at his notes, as though thinking about what she had said. Jessica wished that he would act more enthused about this case but perhaps reserve was an advantage in his profession.

"I'll be honest with you," he said, as the secretary returned with the original, handing it to Jessica. "So far as the boating accident, it would be your word against his as to whether he deliberately abandoned two people in need of help."

"But that's why I need an attorney! Someone may have witnessed the accident...." Her voice trailed off as she looked at him. The expression on his face had not changed in spite of her attempt to convince him.

"You said the water was getting rough, that the big boat was the only other one you saw," he spoke the words slowly, studying her face.

"Yes, but there were still a few people on the beach, I'm sure of that. We could at least prove that Barkley's boat was out there, and that he…"

She leaned back in the chair, pressing her lips together, staring across at the grim-looking attorney. In spite of all her mental rehearsals for this conversation, it was not going well. Perhaps she should have let her father-in-law intervene after all. But she was the one in the water who had screamed to Barkley for help; it was her story and she should be the one to press charges.

Martin McCormick removed his glasses and ran a hand over his forehead, looking frustrated.

"Please understand," he said at last, "I am most sympathetic with your situation. You've obviously been through a terrible ordeal. It's just that we can't take a man as powerful as Barkley to court without something more concrete."

For the past few minutes, she had sat silently, trying to decide if she was making sense or merely babbling. Now, she realized it didn't matter which approach she took; this man had already made up his mind about the case. She refused to waste any more time trying to convince him otherwise.

She came to her feet, hooking her shoulder bag over her arm.

"Mr. McCormick, I don't care how powerful you and other local attorneys think the man is. He could have saved my husband's life, and he didn't. Perhaps I should look beyond this city for counsel. As you say, Jack Barkley is an important man here," she added emphatically.

She allowed her eyes to convey the rest of the message. *And you're afraid of him.*

Before she reached the door, he was on his feet, catching up, gently touching her arm.

"Wait, please," he smiled weakly. "Let's talk about this some more. I've been told I'm a bit too forthright. It's just that I don't want to waste your time. You can find attorneys who will keep you coming back for more consultations and make offers to hire detectives to interview everyone along the beach."

He released her arm and shrugged lightly. "That isn't my style. However," he turned, looking back at his desk, "let me study that contract some more. And let me mull over what you have told me, make some phone calls." He looked back at her. "I'm not ruling out the possibility that we can take him to court and win. I just want to know what we're getting into before we start."

That sounded fair to Jessica and she began to nod in agreement. At least here was a man willing to be honest with her; she should be grateful for that.

"All right," she agreed. "Think it over and give me a call. But you understand I'm running out of time. And money," she added, dropping her gaze.

"I understand," his voice softened. "And there will be no fee unless I take the case, and then I'll only require a percentage of the amount we win, should we file a suit against him."

There was a look in his eyes that had not been there before, and Jessica smiled up at him, grateful that he had not charged her for the advice he had given today.

"Thank you, Mr. McCormick," she said with a smile. "I'll be waiting for your call."

She left his office with mixed emotions. She hadn't expected this to be easy, and yet she hadn't expected it to be so difficult to persuade an attorney to represent her against Jack Barkley.

Stepping on the elevator, she punched the button and forced a half smile at the elderly black woman riding down with her. Jessica took a deep breath and tried to think positively. She had told her attorney the truth, and she had to believe that eventually the truth would win out.

At that precise moment, Martin McCormick was speaking about the matter of truth, in another telephone conversation.

"She claims she's telling the truth, Harold," he argued, "so you'd better look into it." He closed his eyes, momentarily hating himself for what he was doing. But he owed Jack Barkley a favor, a big one. And he had just been reminded of that fact in rather cruel terms by Barkley's chief attorney. "I know and I don't want to oppose him," McCormick said, sighing deeply. "But if I don't take her case, someone else will. And while it's doubtful she could win, she can certainly stir up some bad publicity."

Jessica's spirits lifted as soon as she turned into the driveway and saw her house, glistening like a pink seashell in the bright sunlight. Clarence had completed the cupola and finished the painting. Now he was in the process of touching up the white trim on all the windows and doors.

She got out of the car, her hands on her hips, her eyes moving slowly over the exterior of the house. She was like a doting mother, hovering over a child that needed extra care, but she felt a surge of satisfaction on seeing the results of all that care.

The purchase of swings and rockers would be next. Flower boxes...

Mentally, she ticked off the next phase of her plans, but then suddenly she came up short with the ever-present knowledge that she was almost out of money.

She took a breath and tilted her head back to look at the roof. The cupola added a touch of class to the house, and seeing it, she told herself to focus on all that was going right. There were enough negatives in her world; she had to keep her mind fixed on the positives.

As she hurried up the walk, she glanced around, noting that Clarence's old truck was gone. He'd probably returned to town for more paint.

She opened the screen door, which no longer creaked, and entered the hall, enjoying the aroma of the dried-flower sachet, sent from the mountains. She had dispersed it freely and it now blessed the house, wafting a fresh aroma that was pleasant without being overpowering.

Maybe things would work out, after all. Martin McCormick was an important attorney, and he had been very kind today, refusing to charge a fee for the consultation.

Kicking off her heels in the living room, she followed her nose back to the kitchen, thinking how nice it was to have someone sharing the house with her.

"Ready for lunch?" Wilma called pleasantly as Jessica poked her head in the kitchen door.

"You bet. Wilma, you're an absolute angel." Jessica looked at the table, set with soup bowls, cups and a pot of tea.

Wilma was an avid tea drinker, which suited Jessica.

"Hope you like my conch chowder," Wilma's eyes twinkled as she served up the chowder and they sat down at the table.

"I promise I will love it." Jessica glanced at the older woman and counted her blessings again for having this woman in her life. Wilma was pleasant and helpful, and she had been wonderful to jump in and do whatever was needed. She actually seemed to enjoy hard work, which made Jessica wonder if the heavens hadn't opened up and dropped an angel on her doorstep.

"Wilma, I want to tell you again how much I appreciate what you're doing for me." Jessica smiled at her, then dipped into the thick chowder.

"It's been my pleasure. I appreciate your letting me have a part in Seascape. I now have something I can dive into, use up all my nervous energy, soothe my mind." She smiled, crinkling the skin around her eyes. She had the look of one who had lived well and laughed often. "By the way, Clarence ran home to get some snapshots."

Jessica arched an eyebrow. "Snapshots?"

Wilma's eyes twinkled. "Of his grandchildren. I was telling him about Rob and Katie, my grandchildren in Vancouver. He has four scattered around Florida."

"Oh." Jessica managed to suppress an amused smile.

"He said to tell you he's taking a quick lunch hour," Wilma added, reminding Jessica of how often she had prodded Clarence to watch his time. "He's a funny man," she smiled again, staring out of the window.

Jessica glanced curiously at Wilma. Was it possible that Wilma and Clarence had a little romance going? She had noticed the way the two launched into conversation at every opportunity. They were about the same age and both were alone. Clarence had lost his wife to cancer three years earlier.

Jessica had overheard Wilma and Clarence comparing the illness of their loved ones earlier in the week. She was glad they had found companionship in each other and were able to talk about their losses.

The flavor of the chowder was marvelous, and Jessica examined it with new interest. "What's in this, Wilma? It's terrific. Think I could talk you into serving it to our guests sometime?"

Wilma beamed. "I'd love to! Let's see, I put in bits of left-over grouper fillet, potatoes, tomatoes, and a few of those wonderful spices up there," she tilted her head, indicating the cabinet.

"The leftover grouper?" She gripped Wilma's arm. "Perfect! We can serve fresh fish in the evening and chowder for lunch the following day."

"Good idea! Of course, we're assuming there will be left-over fish. I suppose you could allow a bit for the chowder. It wouldn't be wasteful if you knew it was going to be the cen-terpiece for lunch."

Jessica nodded, appreciating Wilma more than ever. "Right."

"Oh, I almost forgot." Wilma's eyes darted to a notepad on the counter by the phone. "You had a phone call around eleven. I wrote the name down. Mark, I believe it was. He didn't give a last name."

Jessica grinned. "There's only one. I mean, I know only one Mark here." Her heart was beating a bit faster, and sud-denly the chowder and the tea tasted even better.

"Is this the young man you saw on Saturday evening?"

Jessica nodded, wondering if she should share what she was thinking. Wilma's eyes encouraged her, and she began to relate everything, beginning with their meeting on the beach.

"He's really a nice guy," she said, as she finished the story. "In fact, he's the nicest guy I've met in a very long time. I'm glad he called." Her eyes drifted to the phone. "I was afraid I might have scared him off Saturday night when I went ballistic at the mention of Jack Barkley."

Wilma laughed at that. "You, ballistic? I'm sure he can see what a sweet person you are."

Jessica stared into her tea, thinking about her last conversation with Mark. "Well, I shouldn't have gotten off on the subject of Barkley because I become rabid when that man crosses my mind."

For the first time all day Wilma frowned. "You'd be justified in that, I'm sure. Did you tell Mark about —" she broke off, wondering if she should mention Barkley in connection with the boating accident.

Jessica shook her head, taking the last bite of chowder then touching a napkin to her lips. "No. I mentioned that I think he's a crook, but I didn't go into...the rest of it. I was getting upset, and it seemed selfish of me to be talking about my past and ruining our evening. I just let him know how I feel about Barkley. Mark doesn't know him. Well, I believe he said he knew of him, or something like that."

She lifted her eyes and glanced across at Wilma. "See, I'm getting angry again. Anyway, I warned Mark to steer clear of the man. Mark is new to the area and doesn't know many people."

Wilma was listening attentively, sipping her tea. "What

did you say Mark does for a living?"

Jessica stared into space, trying to remember. "He's been trying to decide whether to take a job here and stay on. He has a law degree and—"

"Then you should hire him to represent you!" Wilma beamed at her, thinking this could be the perfect arrangement.

Jessica stared at Wilma, turning those words over in her mind. Then she began to shake her head. "I have no doubt he knows the law, but I need an attorney who has been in a lot of legal battles, who knows people here."

"You're right. Anyway, Mark sounds like he'll be a good friend for you."

Jessica nodded, glancing at the phone. "Did he leave a number?"

"No, he didn't. He said he was going to be out for a while, that he would call you tonight."

Hearing that, Jessica's spirits lifted and she began to hum softly as she and Wilma cleared the table and began to wash the dishes.

Mark was not having a good day; in fact, he was wrestling with a major conflict; more than one conflict, actually. He had been in another conference with Barkley and his attorneys, and now he must make a decision. Did he stay on, enter into a legal agreement that would bind him to the Barkley Corporation?

He was slumped in the desk chair, his elbows on the desk, his large hands massaging his temples. He was trying to press away the drumbeat in his head, for he could feel a migraine coming on, and he didn't have time for it.

Reluctantly he reached into the desk drawer for the prescription bottle, uncapped it and dropped a pill into his hand. With a bracing sip of coffee to wash down the medicine, he returned the bottle to the drawer and leaned back in the chair.

He had more than one decision to make, but the most pressing one was his future with Jack Barkley. What was he going to do? If he took over the company, he could turn things around, make a difference in the lives of those who had been treated unfairly. Like Jessica Thorne.

Don't think about her now, he warned himself. *Stay on track with the first big hurdle.*

He stared at the phone, almost reached for it, then caught himself. He wanted to call his mom, discuss the offer with her. But he couldn't. And his dad had flown to Cincinnati on a business trip. They had warned him when he set out on this emotional journey a year ago that he might end up regretting it. They were right, of course; they were always right. He had never regretted a decision so much in his entire life. Nor had he ever been so tormented and confused.

There was no point in calling them, for he knew what they would say. This had to be his decision. He had their blessings and their love, regardless of what happened. Of course, they had warned him that he was stepping into deep water, but he had been full of curiosity and enthusiasm and youthful optimism. Or ignorance. Yep, he was pretty ignorant about life even if he had graduated magna cum laude and landed every job he'd ever tried to get.

He sighed, closing his eyes. The past week had thrown all of his intelligence back in his face and he suddenly felt like a bumbling idiot. For he had been given a close look at the ugly side of business, the loopholes in contracts, the shark-infested waters of deals and big money. He'd seen it all quite clearly the past week. And he didn't like the view.

A quick rap on his door brought his head up, and he clenched his teeth at the pain that erupted from sudden movement.

"Come in," he called. His voice held a tone of strength and confidence that was a blatant lie about his feelings. In fact, he seemed to be wading in lies lately.

The door was thrown back and the man who had been dominating his thoughts for the past hour walked into the room. For a moment, Mark merely stared, offering no greeting.

Jack Barkley seemed to have aged even more over the weekend, and now as Mark's eyes followed him across the room, Mark wondered what was wrong this time. A hangover? Pills? The man looked terrible, and he walked as though he had weights on his ankles.

"Good morning," Barkley spoke slowly, taking a deep breath that set off a spasm of coughing. Quickly, he reached into his pocket for a linen handkerchief, covering his mouth as the coughing deepened.

Mark leaned forward. "Can I get you some water?"

Barkley shook his head. The gray skin on Barkley's face now held a tinge of color, but this was not a normal color, merely a rush of blood from the spasms racking his body.

Concerned, Mark watched the man sink into a chair and endure the racking coughs until finally there was no sound other than a lingering rasp.

"Are you okay?" Mark asked.

Barkley nodded, replacing his handkerchief and turning his attention to Mark. "You know, you look very much like her."

The words thudded like bricks into a pit of silence. Mark's hands locked over the arms of the chair, gripping hard. He didn't want to hear this, particularly today.

"She was a beautiful woman, but a very selfish one," Barkley continued, as his sunken eyes moved to the window, lifting to the skies beyond. He seemed to be seeing her face out there in the clouds, and for a moment, a different expression filled the faded eyes. But then his features hardened again and his eyes shot back to Mark. "She was determined to be an actress. And obviously, she wasn't going to let anything stop her. Not even you."

A heavy sigh shook Mark's tall frame. "I'm not in the mood to discuss her today." There was an edge to his voice but he couldn't help it. "I'm getting a migraine. I hate them, I fight them, but—"

"You too?" Barkley interrupted, as an odd smile worked over his wrinkled lips. "I have a medicine that works but it always knocks me out."

Mark nodded slowly, glancing back at the drawer. "Same with me. And I just took a pill. I didn't want to, but—"

"Take the rest of the day off," Barkley ordered, the sharp note of command returning to his voice. "I'll cancel the one o'clock conference."

"No. There's no need to do that." Mark came to his feet, towering over Barkley. "I'll be all right."

Barkley's eyes swept up and down the tall, broad-shouldered man with a look of admiration. "Then we'll go on with the meeting," he said, allowing Mark to call the shots. That

odd grin still lingered on Barkley's grey lips. "Migraines…
and just as stubborn," he mumbled, shaking his head.

Through the pounding headache and the blurring vision,
Mark stared hard at the man opposite him who enjoyed
making comparisons and identifying traits he could relate to
and identify.

Mark sank into the seat, saying nothing more. Yet, as he
looked across at Jack Barkley, he found it almost impossible
to believe that this man had fathered him.

Ten

Jessica sat on the edge of her bed, staring at the white telephone on the nightstand. Mark had not called back. She reached out, hesitated, dropped her hand in the lap of her gown. She had been repeating this process for the last five minutes. It was not her style to do the calling, where a guy was concerned, and yet she couldn't help wondering what he wanted and now why he hadn't called back. She had a reason for calling him before — to thank him for the painting. Now there was no reason, other than to say, *What did you want when you called today?*

She forced her hand toward the lamp instead, turning the switch. She crawled under the comforter and stretched her long legs, allowing her mind to be soothed by the comforting rhythm of the ocean.

After lunch, she and Wilma had spent the afternoon polishing the furniture that had finally arrived. She was surprised at how well it fit the house, offering an eclectic mix of modern and antique.

Weariness settled over her, creeping into every muscle

and bone. Her dark lashes drifted down and soon she was fast asleep.

Mark, on the other hand, was not finding sleep as easy. He had come to the beach to think things over and stood now on the balcony of the condo, staring at the dark ocean. The freshening wind was tugging at his cotton pajamas like a playful child. He leaned over, planted both hands on the railing and closed his eyes, letting the cold breeze whip through him. Amazingly, the night wind, loaded with salt spray and a whiff of seaweed, had done more than the medicine to chase away the migraine.

He had stayed in town until late, meeting with Jack and his attorneys. Still, they had not come to terms.

He straightened, plowing his hands through his hair, shoving it back from his face. Inhaling deeply, he lifted his eyes to the starry sky and prayed for direction, and for the man who had led such a troubled life. He could not think of him as a father; no, he could never think of him that way. At the very most, a friend, perhaps. In the beginning, it had been difficult even to like the man, and his first impulse had been to hightail it back to Birmingham.

But something had held him back. Not something. Someone. His eyes lingered on the starry heavens as he released a deep, weary sigh. He didn't see how he could commit himself to take over the company. Jack had installed him in an office of his own while he looked over the ledgers, met the personnel, tried to learn the workings of the huge corporation.

Still, the reason Mark wanted no part of it was the same

reason the beautiful woman at the end of the beach was so miserable. Jack had ruined many lives, and even though Mark might eventually be able to save some people, make things better, he just didn't feel old enough or wise enough to take over.

He had been vaguely conscious of a thumping somewhere, and he turned, glancing through the open glass to the living room. Was someone knocking on his door?

Frowning, he stepped inside, glancing at the clock as he stretched his long legs toward the door. Through the peephole, he could see Walter Gamon, still in his business suit, his hair awry from the night wind.

While unlocking the door, Mark asked himself why Walter had driven all the way out here. What was up?

The door swung back and Walter flooded him with apologies. It was late…he should have called…felt the need to speak with Mark privately.

Still addled from the migraine, the medicine, and a day that had been far too traumatic, Mark tried to summon his manners and invited Walter inside.

"What's up?" he asked, as Walter charged toward the living room.

Walter, second in command at the Barkley Corporation, was a small thin man who radiated nervous energy. Even the air around him seemed charged with electricity as he paced, glancing desperately toward the kitchen.

"You want some coffee, Walter?" Mark asked, interpreting the man's unspoken wish. He knew Walter relied heavily on caffeine to keep him going.

"Please."

Mark headed for the kitchen, recalling how Walter drank

pots of coffee throughout the day. *No wonder he's so wired,* Mark thought, even though he had decided to indulge him. After all, he had driven over here at this late hour and would have to drive back. Automatically, Mark went through the motions of making the coffee as his mind began to clear and now his eyes sought Walter, circling the living room.

"Relax, Walter," he called to him, flipping the switch on the coffee-maker. "You're working yourself up to a cardiac arrest one of these days. You need to take up a hobby."

"Look, Mark," he had decided to come right to the point, "there's something you don't know about Jack."

Mark lifted an eyebrow as he crossed the living room and sank onto the sofa. "Walter, I'm sure there's a lot I don't know about him, but I can tell you this. Nothing he's done would surprise me."

Walter nodded stiffly, then fell into a chair. "Jack's done some things, but he's paying now. Believe me."

Mark studied the little man who knew Jack Barkley better than anyone else. A heavily lined face and bags over and under his gray eyes aged him beyond his fifty-seven years. He was twice divorced, with two adult children living in other states. He ate, slept, and breathed his work.

"Mark, I'm going to tell you what Jack won't. His pride would choke him to death before he begged. He has never asked anyone for anything and never will." He grabbed a breath. "After you walked into his office and told him who you were, he had his doubts. You know how thoroughly he checked you out. When he discovered you really were his son—"

"Wait," Mark put a hand up. "I may be his son biologically, but there's a guy in Birmingham, Alabama, who calls me

Son. And I can assure you, Walter, that man is my father in every way that counts."

Mark's firm tone of voice put Walter on edge. He pursed his lips to shut off an angry retort and weighed his mission here. The undertow of cynicism in his personality threatened to surface, but he forced himself to keep cool. He dropped his eyes to his small hands, turning them over, inspecting them carefully. He owed it to Jack, and that was why he had come.

"All right, we'll let that go for now," he finally responded. "I didn't drive all the way out here to discuss fathers and sons."

Mark frowned. "Then why did you come, Walter? Why do you want me underfoot? You can run the company. No doubt, you have for years. It's obvious the old man is being swallowed up by his bad habits—"

"He's being swallowed up by cancer!" Walter erupted.

Mark felt as though Walter had just landed a sledgehammer in the pit of his stomach. He leaned back against the cushions, trying to absorb the blow.

"What?" he managed to ask, staring at Walter.

"You hear him coughing, you see his skin color. Thought you might figure out the clock is ticking on him. But since you seem to be backing away, I want you to know the truth. If you sign the forms and inherit the company, you'll be running it on your own in two or three months."

Mark stared at the little man whose eyes held a sheen of tears before he quickly dropped his head to study the carpet.

"That...soon?" Mark rasped.

Walter nodded. "Lung cancer in the final stages. Nothing can be done." Slowly, he lifted pain-filled eyes to Mark. "For the first time in the twenty years that I've known Jack, he cares about someone other than himself. And he wants to end his life on a positive note. When you walked into the office and he found out you really were his son, he changed. Completely. He wants to give you the company. Why don't you let him? You'll be a multimillionaire overnight."

There was no sound in the room, other than the gurgle of the coffee-maker as it finished making coffee. Slowly, Mark came to his feet and headed for the kitchen. He opened the cabinet door and grabbed two mugs. As he poured the coffee, he thought of what Walter had just said to him, and suddenly this astounding news changed everything.

Walter had taken a stool at the eating bar and was watching Mark curiously as he filled the mugs with steaming coffee and handed one to Walter.

"It isn't the money," Mark sighed. "You probably think I'm lying about that, but you see, I happen to believe that I have enough ambition and intelligence to make my own fortune. And I intend to make it honestly."

Walter nodded, gulping the coffee. "Okay, I'll buy that. But it'll take you half a lifetime to build yourself a corporation like the one you'll inherit. And if you want to play honest, you can. You can turn the company around, he already told you that. Make amends, if it will soothe that big conscience of yours."

Mark's green eyes shot to Walter, hearing the sarcasm in the older man's tone. Watching Walter over the rim of his cup, Mark chose to ignore the cynicism that often lurked in the man's words. He knew Walter was upset and trying to do the best he could in this situation. He was privately negotiating on Jack's behalf, negotiating for the son he never knew.

His mind returned to the subject at hand. "Walter, I would not take over the corporation for the money," he repeated firmly, looking the man squarely in the eye. "I would do it because...maybe it's the right thing to do. I don't know." He shook his head. "I had made up my mind to say no and head back to Alabama. But I know the fine print in those Barkley contracts has wrecked too many lives. If I can help some people...and Jack, as well...."

He sipped the coffee, thinking it over.

"Mark, it's the very least you can do," Walter argued. "When Jack's gone..." his voice wavered for a moment. Then he plunged on. "You could always sell the company, if you decide you don't want the hassle. You wouldn't have any trouble finding a buyer."

Mark listened, thinking that suggestion had merit. He could sign the papers, take over the company, do the best he could while making an old man's last days peaceful. His eyes drifted through the open door to the starry heavens and he began to nod. A gentle peace washed over him; it was the first time he had felt at peace in quite a while. He knew Walter was right.

He placed the mug on the counter and extended his hand. "Thanks, Walter. You haven't been thinking of yourself in this, I know that. And I'll do the best I can for Jack...and for you."

As the week slipped by, Jessica kept wondering why Mark hadn't called back. It was Thursday and she had hoped to hear from him before the weekend so that maybe they could make some plans. She was thinking as she put the final coat of white paint on the flower box how nice it would be to have dinner and a long chat with Mark. Her eyes drifted across the old table, covered in newspapers spattered with paint, to Wilma who was admiring their handiwork.

Wilma smiled. "Clarence did a good job building these flower boxes."

"Yes, he did." Jessica glanced toward the back of the house, suddenly feeling very good about the way things were shaping up. What she did not feel good about was the fact that Mr. McCormick still had not called her. With the threat of foreclosure looming over her head, time was running out.

"I can just see these boxes, tacked up there under the windows, overflowing with geraniums," Wilma said pleasantly. "Tom and I loved working in our yard."

Jessica glanced at Wilma and saw the sadness in her eyes before she looked away.

"You must miss him terribly," Jessica said gently.

Wilma nodded, toying with a geranium. "I do. But life goes on." She took a deep breath and looked back at Jessica. "I'm proud of the girls. They've turned out well." A tiny frown puckered her brow. "I worry about Robin. She was the middle child and always seemed to have a burr in her shoe." She looked at Jessica and smiled. "She's always had a case of wanderlust. She's the middle child, though, and I'm told they tend to be more independent."

Jessica arched an eyebrow. "I don't know. I'm the baby. Where did you say Robin lives?"

Wilma sighed. "She's in Charleston now. She graduated from college three years ago, and she's been in a different city each year. She wanted to spend some time in the South, so that's why she took a job in Charleston. I spoke to her on the phone last week, and she doesn't know where she'll be next year. It worries me. Having been a teacher myself, I know she needs to get planted in one place."

Jessica smiled. "I'm sure she'll find the right place." She leaned back and removed her work gloves. "I wonder what time it is."

"Around four, I'd guess. We've been out here at least an hour."

Jessica nodded, jumping to her feet. "I going in to call Mr. McCormick. I have to know what's going on with the lawsuit."

"Good idea," Wilma nodded.

As Jessica hurried to the house, she was thinking about her in-laws who had phoned to say they had been called back to Boston for a few days. An elderly aunt had died. Jessica had expressed her sympathy about the aunt, but she thought a trip back home would be good for them. At first, she had felt a sense of relief to have some privacy for a week. Of course, she had felt instant guilt once the thought registered. In the past hour, though, she had begun to wish them back. After all, she would have to ask them for money soon; she had no choice.

She entered the kitchen and hurried to the sink to wash her hands, thinking over what she would say to Mr. McCormick. Taking a deep breath, she dried her hands and reached for the wall phone. She was able to get through to him on the first try, and now she went over the words she had rehearsed. She needed to know something about the Barkley matter.

There was a pause on the other end. Then Mr. McCormick's voice came back to her, low and ominous.

"Jessica, I've checked into this and I don't think we stand a chance in taking Jack Barkley to court. It'll be your word against his, and he might supply a witness to back up his story, whatever it is…"

"How do you know he'll deny it?" she asked foolishly then bit her lip. "Or rather, what would his excuse be for—"

"There was a storm coming up; the flag was flying on shore, warning all boats in. He will claim the negligence was on your husband's part." A heavy sigh filled the air. "Jessica, he has the money to put up a hard fight."

"And I don't," she lashed back. "It isn't fair."

She stared through the kitchen window to Wilma, looking so peaceful and content. Then her vision of Wilma blurred as hot tears stung her eyes and fresh hate for Barkley filled her heart. "The man can do anything he wants and get away with it," she cried, knowing she must sound childish to the sophisticated attorney. Well, she didn't care.

Her fingers wound nervously around the telephone cord while her mind groped for answers. "Surely something can be done," she said, desperate to convince him.

"I have obtained an extension on your deadline," McCormick came back smoothly. "Given the, er, circumstances, they've agreed to give you another six weeks to catch up on your mortgage payments."

The air swished out of her lungs, as relief swept over her.

"Well, that's something," she conceded. And yet this reprieve did nothing to alter her aversion to Barkley.

"Jessica, maybe this extension will give you time to get your place going. Will you be ready to open soon?"

She nodded, lifting a hand to brush away a tear. "Yes."

"Then I suggest you get on with your life, put the past

behind you. That's my best advice, Jessica. If you disagree, you're free to pursue counsel elsewhere."

Jessica closed her eyes, hearing the good-bye in his words.

"Thanks for your help. Just send me a bill," she said.

"My wife and I enjoy driving over to the beach occasionally. Perhaps you can settle the debt with a Sunday morning breakfast some weekend. We'll give you advance notice, of course."

Her first customer for breakfast. "Sure," she began to nod her head. "That's a deal. And I'll be expecting your call."

As she hung up the phone, she remembered the Castlemans would be guests some weekend, as well. Two more customers.

Free legal advice, a free painting that had created the perfect mood for her upstairs. Leaning against the cabinet, she crossed her arms and took a long breath, thinking the situation over.

Maybe she wasn't doing too badly after all.

Eleven

On Saturday morning, Mark picked up the phone and dialed Jessica, wishing he hadn't let the week get by without calling her. He had intended to look up her contract at the office, check into the fine print. But the entire week had been a major crisis for him, and there had been little time to think of anything beyond the mountains of papers from the attorney.

Her soft voice came over the wire, reminding him that he had missed seeing her. He was going to be disappointed if she turned him down.

"Hi, Jessica, this is Mark."

"Hi, Mark. How have you been?"

Her tone was pleasant; she didn't seem to mind that he hadn't called. Thank God, she was not the insecure type who got bent out of shape when a guy was slow in calling back.

"I've been busy, too busy," he sighed. "How's your house coming along?"

"Really well. I'm anxious for you to see it."

He smiled to himself. That was definitely an invitation, so

he decided to proceed with his question.

"Sure, I'd like to see what you've accomplished this week. As a matter of fact, I called to invite you to dinner if you don't already have plans. I apologize for calling at the last minute but the week got away from me."

"That's okay. I'm free, and I'd love to have dinner with you. Wilma is going someplace with Clarence and I have the house to myself. In fact, why don't you come a little early? I'm anxious to show you what we've done."

"I'll look forward to it." Then another thought occurred to him, and he decided to go ahead and try for the afternoon, as well. "Jessica, how would you like to drive down to Seaside this afternoon? We could browse around the shops and then have dinner."

"I'd love to! I've been wanting to go back but haven't had a chance."

"Okay. You name the time. I'm free all day."

She hesitated. "Three o'clock?"

His smile widened. This was even better than he had hoped.

"Great! I'll see you then." As he hung up, he had to restrain himself from thanking her for being so nice.

Mark sank back on the sofa, his hands thrust behind his head, as he stared through the glass doors to the ocean. As he got to know her better, he liked her even more. In fact, he already knew that he liked Jessica Thorne more than anyone he'd ever met.

Then, like a thundercloud hovering overhead, he recalled the angry words she had spoken about Jack Barkley. He grimaced. Telling her would not be easy, but he had to do it. He had signed the papers and officially taken over the Barkley

Corporation. There would be a formal announcement next week. A photographer from the newspaper had already been in to take pictures of Mark and Jack, while the legal department prepared a news release.

At times, he still had conflicting emotions about being CEO of the Barkley Corporation. He couldn't get used to the title that would be his. Ultimately, though, there seemed to be only one decision he could make. God had led him toward that decision, one that he hoped would change and improve the lives of many people.

His thoughts circled back to the newspaper reporter. Yep, he had to tell Jessica. And he had to do it tonight before she heard it elsewhere, before she saw it in the paper.

He swung his long legs onto the coffee table and tried to think through how he would phrase it. He would begin by explaining that he was adopted, that he had always felt a longing to trace his roots, settle the question mark in his mind. She seemed an understanding person; she would be reasonable about this. After all, he couldn't help what Jack Barkley had done in all the years before Mark walked into his office and identified himself.

Having thought it through, he felt better about everything. Pulling himself up, he decided to go for his morning run. He smiled to himself as he hurried to put on his jogging suit. He was sure Jessica would understand.

Jessica had chosen blue linen slacks and a pale blue shirt for her afternoon with Mark. The soft blue of the blouse set off her dark hair and eyes and complemented the tan she had acquired from hours of yard work. As she slipped her feet into navy flats and surveyed her reflection in the wall mirror, a mood of happiness filled her. She turned on the radio and began to listen to a love song. She smiled, thinking of Mark Castleman.

She really liked him, there was no denying it. How did he feel about her? She checked herself in the wall mirror one last time.

The young woman who stared back at her showed no signs of the tumultuous year she had endured — well, almost a year, although it seemed more like ten. She would have expected to have seen deep wrinkles on her forehead from the burden of worries she carried in her brain, and sunken eyes, or at least heavy shadows underneath her eyes, from a hundred sleepless nights. But her forehead contained only one faint line, and her eyes were clear and bright, with no underlying shadows.

At last she was going to have a day of relaxation and fun, her reward for a week of hard work.

She opened her jewelry box and surveyed her small collection. Her eyes fell on the earrings she had worn to the attorney's office, and suddenly she was thinking of Mr. McCormick. The man was right. She needed to get on with her life, put the past behind her. That was the healthy thing to do; still, anger smoldered deep in her soul, like a stubborn fire that refused to go out. The anger had begun to surface at odd times, catching her by surprise. She had snapped at Clarence and immediately regretted it, but he had the gift of gab and he tended to forget they were on a deadline here. She had reminded him of that rather pointedly this week.

The clerk at the drugstore, more interested in conversation with a co-worker than in ringing up a sale, had gotten a scowl from Jessica. And an elderly driver had been the recipient of a piercing stare. Jessica had chided herself for that, later on.

She gazed at the gold chain gleaming against the velvet lining of her jewelry case. Blake had given her the chain. She wondered which credit card he had used to pay for it.

She heard a car pulling into the driveway and whirled suddenly, dropping one of the silver hoops she had just chosen. Kneeling to the floor to retrieve the earring, she tried to calm herself. Spending time with Mark again was exactly what she wanted to do. The girls on her floor of the dorm had one important rule — keep the guys guessing. She was too happy to hear from him to play it cool or keep him guessing, as she would have done in college.

Well, she was past those silly games now, she told herself, hurrying to answer his knock. For Mark Castleman was too nice to be turned down.

"Hi," she smiled, opening the door.

He was wearing tan khakis and a long-sleeved polo shirt. Her eyes moved from the damp strands of his golden-brown hair to the sea-green eyes and she marveled again at how handsome he was. It was the smile that really captivated her — a quick, easy smile, friendly yet sincere. Mark was the most sincere guy she had ever met. She really liked him.

"Hey, I was beginning to wonder if I was at the right place," he teased, shoving his hands in his pockets and turning to survey the porch. "The paint job, the cupola, the trim — it all looks fantastic. Jessica, you've done a super job."

"I think Clarence is the one to be complimented."

"But *you* had the vision."

She smiled. "Yes, I did. Come in. I want to show you

133

something." She opened the door wider and he followed her to the kitchen.

Spread over the kitchen table were black-and-white photos of the porch swings and rockers she hoped to order. "How do you like these?" she asked.

"They look great. I wouldn't mind having a couple of those rockers once I find a house here." The words came out in a rush, and Jessica turned to look at him.

"Then you're staying?"

He grinned. "Yep, looks that way. Where do you get these?" He leaned over the photos, studying the rockers more carefully.

"From a new arts and crafts center that my friend Laurel and her husband Matt Wentworth started this past year. There's some incredible talent up in the Smokies, and Matt had the money and the business sense to provide a building and find markets for the work. It's an interesting story." She turned to the counter and grabbed her shoulder bag. "I'll tell you about it on the way to Seaside."

"A long story, huh?" he grinned.

"Yes, quite long, but fun."

As she locked up and they headed out the door, Mark was shaking his head as he looked around. "I'm still in awe of all you've accomplished. And in such a short time. You'll be ready for tourist season."

"I hope so. I've applied for an operating loan to get me going." She named the bank and tried to keep her voice steady. "I just hope it comes through. Otherwise..."

She pressed her lips together, determined to say no more about her financial problems; she wasn't going to mention Jack Barkley either. She had promised herself she would keep her conversation pleasant and cheerful.

"I was going to tell you about Laurel and Matt," she said, smoothly changing the subject as they got into Mark's car. She began her story about the couple as they drove along at a leisurely clip, enjoying the view while she talked. By the time they reached the outskirts of Seaside, she had detailed everything, including the plane crash.

Mark was slowing down to the speed limit while his mind lingered on the interesting story she had told. "I'd like to meet Matt sometime. He sounds like a great guy."

"He's certainly done a lot for the valley, with Laurel's help, of course."

Mark chewed the inside of his lip, going over the possibilities ahead of him with the Barkley Corporation. He had already begun to think about the good things he could accomplish with Jack's money. Hearing how someone else had done good things for people encouraged him even more.

He opened his mouth, almost ready to tell Jessica what had transpired this week, but instinct silenced him again. An afternoon of fun awaited them. If Jessica didn't react the way he hoped she would, the day would be ruined. It was best to wait until tonight.

"Isn't it pretty here?" she said, lifting a hand to indicate the pastel wood cottages set against the Gulf of Mexico, sparkling green and white in the distance. Sand dunes rose here and there like sugar castles, where children played and adults laughed and frolicked as though all their cares had floated out into the gulf.

"Never saw a post office quite like that one," Mark chuckled, as he searched for a parking space.

135

Jessica smiled, studying the quaint little building. "Looks more like a playhouse than a post office, doesn't it?"

The local post office was a Greek Revival structure of the Thomas Jefferson design, and it perched on the village green surrounded by a lazy plaza of shops.

"We're in luck." Mark came to a stop, waiting for a van to back out of a parking space. When the van had moved on, he wheeled in, cut the engine and looked across at Jessica.

"Well, what's our interest? Art, antiques, books, clothes — you make the call."

Jessica's eyes lingered on the open-air market across the street. "I want to do it all, browse through every shop." She looked back at Mark. "But I realize men aren't as fanatical about shopping as women, so I'll try to be considerate."

Mark shrugged lightly. "I'm game. I told you before, I'm a good sport."

Jessica's dark eyes glowed as she looked at him. "I know. You seem to be a very good sport. Still," her eyes teased him, "maybe I'll put you to the test today. I wore my walking shoes," she lifted a foot to indicate her comfortable shoes.

Mark chuckled. "Okay, where do we start?"

Her eyes drifted toward the corner grocery. "Well, I can never come here without exploring the local market. How about a pastry and tea to get us going?"

"Sounds just right."

They got out of the car and headed for the grocery store which was as unique as any other shop in Seaside. Customers strolled around the aisles, inspecting fresh vegetables, pondering the canned goods that lined neat white shelves, stretching to the ceiling.

Jessica's hand slipped through Mark's arm as they side-stepped shoppers at the gourmet cheese counter and headed toward the exotic coffees and teas.

They ordered pastries and drinks and found a table. "You're about to discover that I'm a professional shopper," Jessica laughed. "No, let me rephrase that. A professional looker." Mark laughed, but Jessica couldn't help wondering if he really was up to tagging around with her to every shop in Seascape. She wanted to hit all of them.

He shrugged good-naturedly. "It's a nice day. Why not?"

Fortified with a snack, they set out to explore the shops, and the hours flew by.

"Have we missed anything?" Mark chuckled as they stood in the center of a Mediterranean-style bazaar. Hours of shopping had merited only one item, which was tucked under Mark's arm.

"I don't think so. I'm glad we found something for your mother."

"With your help."

They had discovered a beautiful little watercolor in one of the shops. When Mark mentioned that the painting looked like something his mother would buy, Jessica had admired his mother's taste.

"Why don't you get it for her?" she suggested.

Mark checked the price and decided it was within his budget. He had been thinking of his mother often during the week, having been told by Jack Barkley that the woman who gave birth to him did not want to be a mother. After giving Mark up for adoption, she had phoned Jack who was in Europe on business and told him the baby was stillborn. Then she had filed for divorce and fled to California.

"You look awfully serious," Jessica's soft voice broke into

his thoughts as he stared vacantly at a display of trinkets.

He turned to Jessica and shrugged, saying nothing. As he looked into her pretty face, appreciating her smile, he suddenly wanted to take her in his arms. He felt like thanking her for being a kind, caring person, but she wouldn't understand. He merely smiled at her instead.

"I'm having a great time," he said, staring into her dark eyes. She was a terrific person, and he found himself imagining her in the role of mother. She would be a wonderful mother, he decided.

"Why are you looking at me like that?" she asked, and her eyes rounded curiously.

For a moment he didn't know how to respond. Then, remembering their purchase, he glanced down at the package under his arm. "Thanks for suggesting that I buy this. Mom has a birthday coming up soon and this will be perfect."

"Glad I could help, although I feel as though I should be the one paying for it. After the painting she sent —"

"We've settled that. Mom and Dad are coming down this fall." He was studying her again as they walked back to the car. "They're going to like you; hope the feeling will be mutual."

"How could I not like your parents, Mark?"

Her voice was soft and tender, and Mark stopped walking and looked at her thoughtfully.

"You know, there's something I'd like to discuss with you."

Jessica stared at him, startled by his serious tone and the sad expression that clouded his features.

"What is it? You look worried."

His eyes swept the crowd around them, the happy faces of Saturday afternoon strollers, the casual chatter. This was neither the time nor the place.

Mark shrugged. "It can wait." They walked on. "I was just going to tell you something about my parents. Remind me to tell you tonight, okay?"

"Sure." Jessica glanced down at the brick-paved walkway. Whatever he was going to tell her was obviously worrying him. Were his parents getting divorced? That was happening a lot nowadays; she was grateful that her parents had built a strong, thirty-year marriage, providing an anchor for Chad and her.

"Well, what'll it be for dinner?" he asked as they reached his car and he unlocked the door.

"Dinner," she repeated, mulling over the possibilities. "It's your call," she teased, giving him the option this time.

"My call," he repeated, depositing the painting in the back seat, then coming around to open her door. "Well, let me give that some special thought. In fact, I should already have reservations at some terrific place, but I don't. Sorry."

"No apologies are necessary. If you had made reservations, we might have been late, considering the fact I wanted to visit so many shops. Besides, I like being more casual about things."

"Glad to hear that. So do I." He winked at her as he closed her door and hurried around to climb under the wheel.

"Mark, thanks for a great afternoon," she said, laying her hand on his arm.

Automatically, he reached for her hand and lifted it to his lips, kissing her palm. The calluses on her skin brushed against his lips, prompting him to hold her hand a few seconds longer. He wanted to help her, protect her, spend hours and hours with her.

He turned her hand over, studying the red places. Embarrassed, she gently withdrew her hand.

"I'm sure my skin must feel like the sandpaper I've been handling all week long."

"Your skin feels wonderful to me," he said, cranking the engine and backing out of the parking space. "Have I told you how much I admire a working gal?"

"Even one with rough hands and paint-splotched jeans?"

He glanced at her and chuckled. "Absolutely."

As he drove slowly through the little town and headed for the highway, Mark was thinking again about her situation at Seascape. "You know, I've never met anyone like you."

"And just what does that mean?" she asked, pretending to be offended while her eyes twinkled.

"I've never known a girl who is as brave and unselfish as you."

"Thanks," she said, feeling embarrassed. She turned to look across a stretch of beach to a yellow Victorian cottage with a latticework tower. "I really like that architecture, don't you?"

"Yes, I do." They drove along in contented silence, admiring the view. Then an interesting-looking restaurant caught Mark's eye and he slowed down.

"Jessica, what do you think of this one?" he asked.

"Looks fine to me."

He pulled into the busy parking lot, and they hopped out and hurried inside, hand in hand. The hostess seated them at a table overlooking the gulf, and Mark leaned back in the chair, staring contentedly at the view. It was exactly what he needed to soothe his mind after the frantic week he had just spent.

"This day just keeps getting better," he said, folding his arms across the table.

Jessica looked across at him, thinking about what a great time she'd had. "I agree."

Their eyes met and locked just before menus were handed to them, turning their thoughts back to dinner. They both decided on a fresh shrimp dish, touted as a specialty of the house. Afterwards, they turned again to the window, watching a fishing boat bobbing lazily out in the gulf. A fiery sun was floating through a sea of white clouds, heading for the horizon.

Mark's eyes drifted back to her. He was developing serious feelings for her, and he didn't know quite what to do about that. He wondered if she thought it was too soon for a relationship; he didn't want to push her so soon after the loss of her husband the past year. Still, he was falling for her, falling hard. She looked up at him with eyes that seemed to say she felt the same, or at least she was certainly interested. Maybe tonight after their conversation about Barkley, he would tell her how he felt about her.

Then he remembered something. He wanted this relationship to be right, and he knew in order for that to happen, he must keep his priorities straight.

"Jessica, I'd like to invite you to church with me again..."

He paused, as the waiter placed huge glasses of minted tea before them, then added salads and dressings to the table.

"I'm starving," Jessica said, dipping her fork into the

salad. She hoped he wouldn't pursue the subject of church; she wasn't ready to go, nor did she want to discuss it.

"So am I." Mark glanced at Jessica. "You didn't answer my question."

"Didn't know you asked one," she quipped, sipping her tea.

"I invited you to church in the morning."

She chewed for a moment, wondering how to phrase an answer.

"What's wrong? Why don't you want to come?"

She dropped her head. "I should come, I know that. I was raised in church. It's just that…" Her eyes wandered toward the spectacular sunset, and she found herself thinking of God.

"Do you blame God for your husband's death?"

"No. My parents taught us to accept death as a part of life, even when it happens to one as young as he was. To be honest, I made some bad choices, but they were *my* choices."

Mark leaned forward, wanting to know what she was thinking. She hadn't come right out and said her marriage was a disappointment, but she had indicated as much. What went wrong?

"Am I being too personal to ask what you mean about bad choices?"

She hesitated. "Marriage may have been a mistake for both Blake and me. I didn't give myself enough time to get to know him before I married him. Then, right away, he seemed to change from the person I thought he was to…someone else. I realize now that we married while we were still in that first level of a relationship."

Mark lifted an eyebrow. "The first level?"

Jessica nodded. "We were still putting our best feet forward, trying to make good impressions. I didn't really know him, and he didn't know me. We were married three months after we met."

Mark shook his head. "I find that hard to believe. You seem so sensible."

"Yeah, well...," she shrugged. "He was a salesman by trade, and he knew how to sell himself, as well." She frowned, glancing at Mark. "My parents liked him, but they tried to persuade me to wait, give the relationship more time." She shook her head. "He invited me to go to Boston to meet his parents, and the first thing I knew there was a diamond on my finger and an engagement party was in progress. It was my one reckless weekend, and I've regretted it many times."

She bit her lip. "I shouldn't have said that. But we both knew we had made a mistake soon after we moved here. We had little in common, and after a while, we discovered we didn't even like each other, to say nothing of love."

Mark reached across the table, squeezing her hand. "I'm sorry. That sounds like a terrible life."

The shrimp was delivered, interrupting this personal moment. Mark was almost sorry he had brought up the subject of Blake, for now it had probably ruined her appetite.

"When you get back home," he said pleasantly, "let's check your calendar and call my parents to come down. I'd like to set up a time before Dad fills all his weekends with football games."

"All right."

Jessica swallowed hard, trying to force the unpleasant memories from her mind. She had escaped from her past, and now she hoped for a better future. Her eyes lifted from the delectable food to Mark's handsome face. The present had certainly improved; in fact, it was wonderful. She had to stop saying such morbid things to Mark; it put a damper on their good times.

She remembered he was going to tell her something about his parents, and she was curious. She was about to ask but decided to forgo that question in favor of another one.

"You mentioned you've decided to stay here. I assume you took that job you mentioned. Where did you say you're working?"

Twelve

For a company in Panama City," Mark answered quickly. "Before I forget to mention it, I'm going to be looking for a place to live." His words came in a rush, and he tried to slow down, appear casual. He wanted to wait to discuss the nature of his work. "The condo is only temporary. Maybe you can help me find something suitable."

This had piqued her interest, handily sidetracking the subject of his job. "What did you have in mind?"

"I'd love to have a little cottage on the gulf, nothing too fancy, just something that would be right for me, something with a nice view." He glanced out at the water, his fork poised over his plate.

Jessica nodded, mulling this over in her mind. "You shouldn't have any trouble finding a place. I'll be on the lookout for something that sounds good. Clarence, my handyman, has lived here for twenty years, and he's quite familiar with the area. I guess he's done carpentry work in half the houses here."

"Good. I'll talk to Clarence. I've seen his work. Maybe he

could help me when he finishes at your place."

"Just don't get into a conversation with him unless you have plenty of time to listen."

They laughed at that as they dined leisurely, enjoying their shrimp; they even shared a luscious chocolate dessert. As they left the restaurant and crossed the parking lot, Mark lifted a palm to press his stomach.

"I'm ready for a walk on the beach. How about you?"

Jessica moaned. "Absolutely."

"Mrs. Vandercamp!" A voice called, repeating the name again.

Jessica turned. Nick LaSorda, manager of the marina where Blake kept his boat, was getting out of a car nearby.

Jessica smiled when she spotted him, but she found herself reluctant to talk with him because he was a reminder of Blake and the boat. Still, Nick was a nice man and she couldn't be rude simply to escape bad memories.

He extended his hand. "How are you doing, Mrs. Vandercamp?"

"I'm okay, thanks. Nick, I'd like you to meet a friend of mine, Mark Castleman. Mark, this is Nick LaSorda. He manages the Gulf Marina."

Mark extended his hand. "How do you do."

"Nice to meet you, Mark." Nick pumped his hand, looking him up and down before the handshake ended. Then Nick's eyes shot back to Jessica. "Well, I just wanted to say hello, Mrs. Vandercamp."

He hesitated, his dark eyes turning sad. Jessica could guess what he was thinking. *I'm sorry about Blake.* She had seen that expression on other faces when people tried to find the right words, then gave up. She decided to make it easy for him.

"It's good to see you again, Nick. By the way, I'm opening my bed and breakfast in a few weeks. You'll have to stop in for a cup of coffee."

He arched an eyebrow. "You're actually going on with that plan?"

She felt like laughing. She knew everyone expected her to hightail it back to Kentucky, and now it gave her a great deal of pride to look Nick in the face and speak confidently. "Yes, and I'm going to make that plan work."

Nick began to nod as his eyes swept her. "I always thought you were a brave lady. You've confirmed it again. I *will* stop in," he said. "Well," his smile moved from Jessica to Mark, "you two have a nice evening."

"Thanks."

Jessica turned back to the car, waiting for Mark to unlock the door. He seemed to be fumbling with his keys, and she glanced at him curiously.

"Something wrong?" she asked, wondering if he disliked Nick.

"I'm just puzzled," he said, inserting the key then glancing at her with curious eyes. "He called you Mrs. Vandercamp. I thought your last name was Thorne."

"Oh, that," she said, getting into the car. "Thorne is my maiden name."

"Oh." He closed the door. As he walked back around to the driver's side, he still looked puzzled.

"Mark," she said, when he got in, "I didn't keep Blake's name because of his bad credit. He was up to his ears in debt, and I knew if I was going to clear the slate and start over, I needed every break I could get."

He nodded again. "Good idea."

147

As he cranked the engine and they drove out of the parking lot, he appeared deep in thought. Jessica decided to tell him everything. They were getting to know each other well now; she didn't want to hold anything back, for she knew he wouldn't.

"You see," she began slowly, "I've had to prove to the merchants here that I am responsible and can run a business. Blake was really irresponsible. He was an only child, accustomed to getting everything he wanted. When he grew up, he simply exchanged little boy toys for big boy toys."

She glanced at the sand dunes they were passing and heaved a sigh, already feeling the weight of bad memories settle over her. Whenever she thought about Blake and their problems, she felt tired to the bone.

"I've told you we were different, that I didn't know him," she continued, speaking quietly. "He was the most irresponsible person I have ever met. He was always chasing dreams but he wasn't willing to dig in and work to make those dreams come true."

The scowl on Mark's face deepened. "He left that work to you," he said, clearly angry.

She reached over, touching his arm. "He had some good qualities —"

"I'm beginning to wonder what they were," Mark interrupted.

Looking at Mark, Jessica was touched by his concern for her. It was nice to see someone getting angry at Blake in her defense. She hadn't allowed herself that kind of luxury, for she had been too proud to admit to her parents just how bad the marriage was. She had bolted to the altar with him while her parents begged her to wait.

She took a deep breath. "Mark, Blake paid for his reckless habits the day he insisted on going out in his boat, in spite of a bad weather forecast. I told him we wouldn't have time to get back before the storm hit. He wouldn't listen, as usual, and foolishly, I went along with him."

Mark whirled toward her, wide-eyed. "You mean you were with him?"

"I thought I should go because he had been drinking too much. He was very reckless...." Her voice trailed off as she dropped her eyes to her hands. "The boat overturned and I'll never, ever forget the look on his face or his desperate cries for help before he went under the last time. I was fighting for my own life — there was no way I could save him."

"Jessica, you're lucky to be alive!" He paled, and again Jessica was touched by his concern.

She felt the tears sting her eyes. "Even though I've told you his faults, I still had feelings for him. He was my husband."

His hand reached out, gripping both of hers. "I'm so sorry."

She sighed. It felt good to talk about her feelings with someone who cared about her. Sue and Mel were always wanting to talk, but of course their feelings about Blake were quite different from hers, and they didn't seem to realize how difficult it had been for her. Before their discussions ended, Sue always started crying and Mel became upset; Jessica ended up being their comforter while wishing she had a strong shoulder to support her.

"The worst part was," she hesitated for a moment, "Blake could have been saved."

Mark squeezed her hand tighter. "Jessica, it's a miracle

you got out alive. I've read accounts of those kinds of accidents."

"Yes, but he might still be alive if only the big boat had stopped. I screamed for help," she said bitterly, "but he just looked right past us and kept going. He was too important to dirty his hands with the likes of us."

Aware that her voice was shaking, Jessica was relieved to see the turnoff to her driveway just ahead. She needed to get out, walk the beach — no, run the beach — to release some of this rage that was overpowering her again.

"Who are you talking about, honey? Who could have saved you?"

She clenched her teeth and inhaled slowly, feeling her nerves relax a bit as she exhaled. She swallowed against a dry throat and looked across at Mark as he slowed down at the driveway.

"Jack Barkley."

Mark hit the brakes with a force that slammed her against the dash. The left wheel struck the curb at the turn-in and Mark spun the wheel again, throwing her against the window.

Her head throbbed from the blow she had taken, but it was not serious. She would be all right. What disturbed her even more was the sight of Mel's van in the driveway. Sue and Mel stood in the yard, gawking at Jessica and Mark.

This was not the way she had planned to introduce Mark to them. She made a valiant effort to recapture her composure while glancing at Mark.

He was as pale as death! What on earth had crossed in front of them, forcing him to slam on his brakes so erratically? She looked back at the yard. There was no time to explore the cause of their near-wreck, for already Mel was stretching his long legs toward them.

"My in-laws," she muttered under her breath.

"Oh no," Mark groaned, looking even worse.

"It's okay, just let me handle it. They're pretty nice. Really." Was she trying to convince Mark or herself? she thought, hearing the tremor in her voice.

Mel stood by the driver's side, glaring at Mark. He looked even more formidable than her father, the night she missed curfew and he met her on the front porch.

She opened the door and hopped out, hurrying around to her father-in-law.

"Mel, I'm so glad you're back!"

"What happened?" he whirled on her. "That guy almost wrecked at the driveway."

"A dog," she said, amazed at her quick lie. "He was fortunate to miss it," she added, glancing back over her shoulder.

Mark was drawing himself to full height, which wasn't quite enough to look Mel straight in the eye, but he tilted his head back and gave it his best shot.

Looking at Mel, Jessica decided Mark was one brave guy not to wilt beneath Mel's thunderous stare.

"Good evening, sir." He extended his hand. "I'm Mark Castleman."

Mel's eyes shot back to Jessica as he slowly held out his hand. Sue had reached her husband's side, eager to assist, protect, or defend. She had become an expert at intervention.

As the men shook hands, both women suppressed a sigh of relief. Then Sue was smiling nervously, her dark eyes sweeping Mark up and down, taking in every detail while being introduced.

"How was your trip? Long and tiring, I'm sure." Jessica gave first Sue and then Mel a quick hug.

"Yes. Too much traffic, as always," Mel complained, staring at Mark.

"Then it's time for tea." Jessica answered. It was an automatic response and the words rolled quickly from her lips.

"That sounds wonderful," Sue cooed, "and we can get to know Mark better."

Those words stopped Jessica cold, and when she looked at Mark, she saw that he had not bothered to fall into step with them.

"Actually," he glanced at his watch, "I can't stay. I'm driving up to Birmingham tomorrow to visit my parents, and I need to do some packing tonight."

Jessica stared at him, recalling his invitation to church. He hadn't mentioned going home then. Was he lying, or had he planned to go after church? Suddenly, she felt heartsick at the way the evening was turning out. Her eyes begged Mark to understand, while she forced herself to say nothing more. If she insisted on his staying, they were sure to grill him, and it was unfair to subject Mark to that. On the other hand, she didn't want him to think their visit was more important than his.

She hesitated, torn over the right response. Then it came to her. "See you at church."

His face was void of expression now. He reminded Jessica of someone who had just survived a terrible shock.

His eyes wandered back from Sue and Mel to Jessica and he began to nod. "Yes. See you then. Nice meeting you folks."

Jessica sneaked a glance at her in-laws as they mumbled a

response. Actually Sue and Mel were good-hearted people, but now they were surveying Mark with obvious suspicion. She bit her lip, wondering if he thought they had been rude. Her eyes followed him as he got in the car, giving them a little wave of farewell, before he backed out and drove off.

Jessica took a deep breath, steeling herself for the questions. Then, impulsively, she decided to beat them to the draw.

"Mark is a friend I met on the beach —"

"On the beach?" Sue fired the first shot.

"He's a very nice guy, perfectly harmless," she added, glancing at Mel. He stood, hands on hips, staring after Mark's vehicle. "His parents will be guests here." She didn't bother saying when. Let them think this had something to do with the friendship.

"Oh," Sue nodded, as though relieved to know that a set of parents were involved in this friendship.

"Come on inside," Jessica said, as the tense ache in her shoulders began to crawl down her back. She had planned to ask them for money when they returned. Now, she wondered if she would ever have the courage to do that.

Money was on Jack Barkley's mind as he poured himself a stiff bourbon and surveyed the trophies on his den wall.

He'd done it all. Safaris in Africa, steelhead fishing in Canada, bears in Alaska. Heads and hides perched and lurked from every corner, meaningless in light of the greatest trophy of his life — Mark. The ice jiggled in his cocktail glass as he shuffled across the huge den, his stubby feet sinking into layers of plush carpet leading to his recliner.

Settling in, he took another belt of bourbon and tried not to wince as the strong liquid burned a path down his raw throat and fought with his queasy stomach. He didn't care if it made him sick. He had to have his bourbon.

Suddenly he met his own reflection in a mirror over the bar and he was stunned. He had always been a small man, stocky and tough, yet what he saw was enough to send him back for another drink. A skimpy little man with oily black hair and sallow skin faced him. Behind the thick-lensed glasses, the eyes were socketed in so much loose flesh that it was hard to detect their color.

What did he care? He had his comforts. His hand shot to the end table, seizing the bottle of painkillers. He hesitated, not yet ready to cloud his mind.

Mark! He wanted to think about Mark.

His hand fell away from the bottle and slinked back to the loose folds of his gray satin lounging robe. Around him, the house was quiet and still, the maid and housekeeper already installed in their bedrooms for an evening of television.

Mark. Cautiously, he took a breath, not a deep breath or a quick one, just a little breath to sustain him. He was careful, gentle, not wanting to bring on a fit of coughing.

He pressed his head into the butter-soft leather of his recliner and thought about yesterday's meeting with Mark and the attorneys.

The two had sat together at the conference table, lawyers at their elbows, papers and pens everywhere, two pots of coffee, a dozen cups.

Mark had looked at him differently. And he had spoken differently, as well; his tone was gentler, kinder. A tiny grin of satisfaction pulled at the corners of Jack's sagging lips.

Money always did that, changed people's tone of voice, the look in their eyes. He had feared Mark was above being compromised for money, but alas — he was human, after all. That was okay, good in fact. Showed the boy knew when to swallow his pride and jump for the deal.

Mark was his son, he had known it almost from the beginning, but ever cautious, he had waited to be sure. Paulette's one redeeming feature was her beauty. Tall and statuesque, she had brown-blonde hair, the exact color of Mark's hair, and vivid green eyes that could stop traffic. Mark had those same eyes. It jolted him sometimes to look at Mark and see Paulette lurking in someone so nice. For beyond her beautiful smile, she had been evil to the core. What, he wondered, had made Mark so good?

And then he remembered his own mother, and he was stunned to feel something warm creeping down his cheek. He raised a weary hand to touch the tear. Good thing he was on his way out; he was turning into a simpering old fool. He could think of at least a dozen enemies who would already be circling if they could see him now.

His mother, Annabelle, had died of cancer when he was only eight, but he still remembered the soft southern voice that never spoke an unkind word. He remembered her gentle hands on his shoulders, the lullabies she sang to him, the hours she read to him. She had been destroyed to discover that her husband, Jack's father, was not only a thief, he was hopelessly addicted to pretty faces, lots of pretty faces.

Jack tried to remember the father who had beaten him half to death on more than one occasion, but the memory of that forgotten man was locked in a dark corridor of his mind, never to return. Just as well — he was content not to be reminded of the man who had shaped his son and daughter into cold, unfeeling individuals.

Jack had thought himself incapable of emotion after feeling a twinge of sadness when first Carol, then Paulette, left him, taking with them a comfortable share of his assets. He had felt even worse upon learning the only son he ever fathered was stillborn.

But that baby was not stillborn, as Paulette had claimed when she telephoned him in Europe. He was here now, ready to take over the company, ready to be with Jack through his last days. And now something wonderful had happened to Jack. He finally knew the joy of a deep, sweet emotion filling his heart. It was a father's love for his son.

He smiled at that, as pride and happiness mingled into sheer ecstasy. He set down his glass without finishing the drink and reached for the phone, thinking there was no point in waiting until next week to break the story. Let the whole world know he had a son, a strong intelligent son. He would be the envy of the lot now, of those who cursed him and wished him the worst.

He chuckled to himself as he dialed the private line of a man he knew well, the owner of the largest newspaper in the area. So what if it already was evening? He'd granted the reporter an interview and pictures, hadn't he? And he knew from past experience that the Sunday edition was not run until the last minute. The Sunday morning paper — everyone enjoyed it. But nobody was going to enjoy it as much as Jack Barkley tomorrow.

"Harry," he barked into the receiver, "you want to spice up that rag you call a paper?"

On Sunday morning Mark dragged himself out of bed and headed for the shower. It would take an hour under a hot spray to get his mind humming again. After a sleepless night, he had surrendered to an exhausted sleep just before daybreak. It seemed like three seconds, rather than three hours, when the nagging buzz of his alarm reached his numb brain.

Circling through the kitchen, he flipped the switch on the coffee-maker and reached for a bottle of aspirin. The astounding words Jessica had spoken last night hit like a hurricane again, and he was still reeling from the damage.

"Don't think about it yet," he muttered, dragging himself to the shower. "I'll deal with it later."

He wasn't sure how; he was praying for a miracle.

He adjusted the shower head to a needling spray to pelt the taut muscles in his neck and shoulders. After five minutes beneath the warm water, and a thorough shampoo, he stepped out and reached for a thick towel.

He dried quickly, then picked up the hair drier. At last, he was awake, his adrenaline pumping, his mind desperately seeking a way to break the news to Jessica after church.

Church would help. Afterwards, she would be more willing to listen to him. Still, it was going to be hard to make her understand things. Before he even tried, he was going to have a talk with Jack.

He gazed into his coffee, wondering what on earth had happened that day in the gulf? How could Jack have ignored two people about to drown? He wouldn't have.

Jack was a heavy drinker; maybe he was drunk that day. It was all he could think of to explain such negligence.

Wrapping the towel around his torso and tucking a corner

at his waist, he padded to the kitchen and reached for a mug. The wonderful aroma of coffee filled the kitchen and he poured himself a cup, sauntering toward the glass wall to survey the ocean. He pulled the cord on the draw drapes and gazed out. A clear and beautiful day had dawned, and the gulf was a green mirror, still and unruffled, a pleasant contrast to his state of mind.

He heard the thump of the newspaper at the door and headed down the foyer to retrieve it. He padded to the eating bar, set down his coffee mug with a yawn, and opened the front page wide to spread it over the bar. Then, suddenly, the picture at the bottom of the page shut off his breath mid-yawn.

There before him was the picture the reporter had taken on Friday, scheduled to accompany an article next week. The picture, and the caption below it, told the world that Mark Castleman, son of Jack Barkley, was the new CEO for the Barkley Corporation.

While residents throughout the Florida panhandle emerged from doorways to grab their papers, only one person was more startled than Mark to pick up the Sunday paper, view the picture, read the caption.

And that person was Jessica.

Thirteen

J essica froze, not even thinking, for a good ten seconds as she stared at the picture in the newspaper.

She had just taken her seat at the kitchen table to sip her tea while her hair dried. She had awakened early, showered and dawdled at the closet, trying to choose the right dress for church. Her search for dress and shoes had been interrupted by hunger pangs, and she had dashed to the kitchen for tea and a bagel slathered with Wilma's homemade apple butter.

The tea and bagel were forgotten, along with everything else, as her mind groped with reality. She held the newspaper only half a dozen inches from her face and stared at the picture. It was Mark, or at least it looked like Mark. The picture was quite clear, but even if it weren't there was no mistaking his identity from the caption underneath.

Her stomach turned as she read the caption.

Mark Castleman, son of Jack Barkley, takes over as CEO of the Barkley Corporation.

Waves of shock rippled through her. Surely this was a mistake. The emotions that followed were slow and languid, like the gentle waves moving into the shoreline below the house. A numbness crept across her brain, cushioning her from further shock. Then followed confusion as she reread the caption, and finally disbelief.

She had never in her life wanted so desperately to believe there was some mistake. It couldn't be true, it couldn't be. And yet, here it was, in black and white, before her startled eyes.

The print was blurring as she gripped the paper with trembling fingers, holding the picture closer.

Mark stood beside...*him*. Jack Barkley, the man she hated more than anyone in the universe. And Mark knew that. And he also knew...

The paper fell from her hands onto the table as she stared vacantly out the window. Tears filled her eyes, flowed down her cheeks, unchecked.

Slowly, her mind made a tortuous journey back over those dates with Mark. She thought back to how she had met him, that day on the beach. He had approached her and tried to start a conversation. She had walked away, then run into him again in the grocery, when she had bumped his cart. Her eyes narrowed. Maybe he had been the one to bump carts.

Her breathing quickened as she recalled how exceptional he had been, how unbelievably nice! She had thought it unusual for a stranger to be so helpful, but she had attributed his kindness to the fact that he was a caring person.

Her mind moved on to the morning he had come over with the twins, and she had admired him in his role as a loving uncle. From there she recalled the dinner dates, the way he had drawn her into conversation. He had kept her talking while revealing little about himself, except for the loving parents in Birmingham! He must have called an art dealer in Birmingham and had them ship the painting, which he claimed to be a gift from his mother.

Grabbing a napkin, she swabbed her cheeks and told herself to quit crying, it would do her no good now. But she could not stop the tears that flowed from a wellspring of hurt. How could he do this to her? And how could she have erred so badly in her judgment, thinking he was the nicest, most sincere guy she had ever met?

Sniffling, she stared again at the caption, blurred by her tears. The answer to her questions lay in the print before her. Jack Barkley's son? Obviously, the son had the genetics to be just as cold and manipulative as the father. Why couldn't she accept that? Why couldn't she believe he was capable of anything, being Barkley's son? The new CEO! So that was it. He was taking over the company; naturally, he wanted to avoid bad publicity for the company, such as a lawsuit and bad press.

She lifted her eyes to the window again, watching the sun disappear behind dark clouds. Her lips were pressed in a grim line as she stared at the sky and thought vaguely that the weather seemed to typify her mood, her very life, for that matter.

Leaning back in the chair, she closed her eyes and tried to summon enough anger to overpower the heartache. She had fallen for a man she didn't know, a man who was every bit as deceptive as her husband. No, he was even worse.

The phone began to ring and she stared at it for several

seconds. Could it possibly be him? Would he dare call her?

She remembered he had invited her to church, and suddenly the entire thing seemed more preposterous than ever. If this announcement was to be Sunday's news, how had he planned to cushion her shock? Had he planned some big lie for last night when they returned home? Then her in-laws had foiled his plan.

Thank God for Sue and Mel. If not for them, she might have been subjected to an evening of romance, with a smooth lie mixed in. She wondered what sort of lie would have blurred the hideous truth, and did he really think she was dumb enough to fall for it?

The phone continued to ring and she decided to answer, thinking it might be her parents. It wouldn't be him. He wouldn't have the nerve to call her now.

Lifting the receiver, she answered quietly. For a moment, there was no response on the other end of the line. Then she heard Mark's voice, low and remorseful.

"Jessica, we need to talk—"

She slammed the phone back on the hook, giving him her answer to that one. She hurried out of the kitchen, leaving behind cold tea and an untouched bagel. She began to devise her strategy as she rushed upstairs and put on jeans and a sweatshirt. She wasn't sure where she was going; she only knew she had to escape for a few hours until she knew what to do.

He would come here; somehow she felt certain of that, although she didn't know what he had planned to say either on the telephone or in person. But he wouldn't get an opportunity to make a fool of her again. Not today, not ever.

Finally, the anger she needed to protect her raced through

her veins, charging her with energy. She ran the brush through her hair and bypassed the makeup. She had locked up the house and was in the driveway within ten minutes after his call. She jumped in her car and drove off, heading toward Panama City. Away from the beach, away from the highway that led to Mark's condominium.

A mile down that highway, Mark was breaking the speed limit to get to her. The temperature was dropping, and the skies promised rain. Through the cracked window, a chilling breeze ruffled his hair and drifted down his T-shirt and jeans. Still, the cold felt good on his flushed cheeks; he hated to think what his blood pressure would register at this moment.

He slowed for a traffic light, his fingers drumming the wheel. He had to see her, talk to her, try to make her understand.

He had already dressed when he telephoned her. His first instinct had been to simply show up at her door and beg to be given five minutes to explain. The reason he had telephoned first was his concern about the Vandercamps still being at Jessica's house. He was unclear, from last night's conversation, whether they lived nearby or had just arrived for a visit.

The light changed and he accelerated again, his mind sorting through questions, answers, solutions. *When did you get back?* she had asked the couple as they gawked at him. They must be staying somewhere in the area. Still, he dreaded another encounter with a man who looked at Mark as though he were an outcast, or worse. So he had telephoned first, and that had been a mistake.

He took a deep breath as he spotted her driveway up ahead. He had almost wrecked when she spilled Jack's name here last night, shocking him so that he had slammed on the brake, rather than merely touching it for the turn.

Mark had thought nothing could be worse than hearing the horrible story about her husband drowning before her eyes. He was wrong. Hearing her speak the name of the man who had sped by without helping them had devastated him. He still had no idea what to do, for Jack wasn't answering the phone; but he couldn't wait any longer to see Jessica and explain why and how he was associated with the man she hated so much.

He slowed down and turned cautiously into her driveway. His heart sank. Her car was gone; she had suspected he might come over and had left. But she'd have to return sometime; he would simply wait. He slumped back in the seat, watching the raindrops falling gently on his window.

Jessica had found a small, out-of-the-way coffee shop in town. She sat in a booth by the window, watching the rain. After an hour, she had finally come to grips with reality. The next step, she knew, was to see Sue and Mel, for there was no telling what they would do. Of course they would be shocked speechless when they saw the Sunday paper. Reading the morning paper was a ritual with Mel, and no doubt he had already opened the front page. She couldn't begin to imagine what he and Sue were thinking; she felt certain they had already telephoned her, or were probably knocking on her door already, which was another reason she had left home. She wanted to get a grip on her emotions before she faced anyone.

She felt as though she never wanted to eat again; but for sustenance, she knew she must try. She stopped at a restaurant and ordered a mild soup but left most of it. Then she drove to Destin and braced herself for a meeting with her in-laws.

Mark had been sitting in the driveway for three hours when finally he gave up the mission. For all he knew, she could have gone to Angel Valley, where she had said her closest friends lived. In any case, after sitting on her porch for hours, he had left a note on her door.

Please believe me, I never meant to deceive you. And please give me a chance to explain what I wanted to tell you.

He had reread the note twice, still feeling it was inadequate. How could he find the right words? Maybe there weren't any.

He took one last look at the house before he drove off. It occurred to him that he might never see the house, or Jessica, again. And that thought bothered him more than anything that had happened all week.

When Jessica arrived at the Vandercamps' condo, she could see the damage was already done.

Sue, looking pale and shaken, met her at the door. Her dark eyes were round with shock, and for once she was at a complete loss for words. Then, opening the door wider for Jessica to enter, she found her voice and a jumble of questions burst from her lips.

"Where have you been? What's going on? Is it true? We've been trying to call and—"

"Who is it?" Mel thundered from behind her.

Sue reached out, grasping Jessica's arm, pulling her down the foyer to the living room.

Mel was slumped in a chair, staring blankly at the television screen, the newspaper strewn about. In the center of the coffee table lay the front page.

Obviously, they had already seen the paper. Coming here had been one of the hardest things Jessica had ever done, but she had no choice. A sense of duty had forced her to speak with them, explain her connection with Mark Castleman.

"Why is his name Castleman?" Sue blurted.

"Jessica," Mel barked, "What in the—"

"Please! Just listen. I'll explain as much as I know."

She took a seat on the sofa, turning to face the man and woman who had suffered a broken heart with the loss of their son. She had to be gentle, yet firm.

She cleared her throat and began her story with that day on the beach when she met Mark. She continued with the incident at the grocery store, then hesitated. She decided to omit the part about her blouse, and even the details of the time she spent with him. She merely said she had seen him a couple of times since, that they had gone shopping yesterday afternoon before they returned home and the Vandercamps met him.

"I didn't like the looks of him," Mel growled.

Jessica said nothing as she looked at him, but she was thinking that his snap judgments and criticisms had always bothered her.

"What about him did you not like?" she asked quietly.

He hesitated, obviously not anticipating that question.

166

"Did you sense he was a deceptive person?" she pressed on, unable to stop herself. She knew she had made a terrible mistake but she was tired of Mel always looming over her, ready to judge and condemn.

His brow lifted as he shot a glance at Sue, seeking an answer.

Sue cleared her throat, taking a seat by Mel. "For one thing, he's a reckless driver," Sue put in.

Silence followed, for they all knew that had no bearing on the problem.

"What about that lawsuit?" Mel asked, frowning at Jessica.

Her heart sank. In the excitement of all that had happened, she had completely forgotten to tell them about her conversation with McCormick. Now she was forced into it with no preamble, and she knew they were not going to like that part either.

She related the conversation as best she could, but she was unable to finish before Mel leapt to his feet, pacing circles around the room.

"That lawyer's been bought off by Barkley!" he thundered.

"Mel, you recommended that firm," Sue reminded him, her tone taking on the slight whine that accompanied Mel's moods.

"Well, it's not the only one in town," he retorted, grabbing the telephone book.

Jessica's eyes moved from Mel to Sue as she took a deep breath, suddenly wishing she had gone to church, after all, though not with Mark Castleman. She was running out of strength on her own, but she tried to calm herself and say what must be said.

"Could you two just listen to me for a minute, please?"

Both heads turned.

"You've had enough to worry you, so I never told you this, but Blake had overextended his credit. He had…" She hesitated, hating to tell them, but she had no choice now. "…run through his savings and he had to choose a mortgage firm that made loans to people who were credit risks. As a result, the interest rates and late charges are higher." She took a breath, trying to still the trembling in her voice. "The contract stipulates that once we accumulate late charges and fall behind two months on the payments, the house can be repossessed."

She watched the horror creep over their faces, draining the color from their skin.

"We have reached that point," she said, dropping her eyes to her clenched hands. "You know the extent of the repairs that were necessary to put the house in shape. The attorney spoke with the Barkley lawyers, and I've been granted an extension on—"

"You sold out!" Mel exploded, the color rushing back to his face as he glared down at her. "You let those crooked lawyers talk you into—"

"Stop it, Mel," Sue cried, jumping to her feet. While she was a tiny woman, once she decided to react, she had a powerful effect on Mel, who closed his mouth and stared at her.

Jessica could take no more. She got up and started for the door, the tears she had held back spilling onto her cheeks. "I've done the best I could under horrible circumstances," she said, glancing back at them. "And I haven't asked you for anything," she added pointedly, before rushing through the door.

She ran to her car and jumped in, wondering if she was in any condition to drive, but she had no choice. She was trembling from head to toe, her stomach heaved, and everything inside her ached. Most of all her heart.

She drove away, her hands clenching the wheel as she fought tears again. That hideous day in the gulf had been the worst day of her life. Today was the second one.

Fourteen

Mark wheeled into the driveway of the estate that stretched across the block. Hopping out, he glanced up at the imposing brick structure, thinking how cold and formal it seemed. Like the man who lived inside.

He sprinted to the front door and rang the bell, his hands shoved deep in his pockets, jingling the loose change. Where was the maid? he wondered, giving the bell another jab. He suddenly remembered the house key Jack had given him, and he dashed back to the car, reaching for the key ring in the ignition. He was back at the door, key extended, when the massive door swung back.

Jack faced him with rumpled hair and glazed eyes behind glasses, slightly askew. He was wearing a lounging robe over pajamas, although it was mid-afternoon.

Seeing Mark, the old man began to smile.

"Mark, come —"

"We have to talk."

Mark charged toward the den. Jack frowned, shuffling along after him.

Mark stood in the center of the huge room, his eyes sweeping Jack's frail frame. Looking at Jack, Mark thought about the cancer eating away at his lungs. He lifted a hand to rub his forehead, telling himself to calm down. This was no way to treat a dying man. But then he remembered another dying man abandoned in the gulf, and his anger rushed back.

"What happened the day you were out in your boat when the Vandercamps' boat overturned? He and his wife screamed for help and you ignored them."

Jack came up short. His sluggish brain stumbled over Mark's words for several seconds while computing the anger in his son's face, the contempt in his eyes.

Years of expertise took over and now Jack's razor-sharp instincts rose to the occasion. He was glad the cancer that ate up his body had not yet touched his brain. His eyes shot to the bar, but he refrained from grabbing a bourbon or offering one to Mark, who always refused.

"I never saw them," he said in a gruff voice.

Mark stared at him. "How could you have not seen them? The boat was overturned, they were yelling for help."

Jack studied Mark's countenance for a few more seconds. He could see the matter was crucial to Mark and that he was angry, very angry. Jack, when cornered, always came out swinging, even if the opponent was the one person in all the world that he loved.

"You think I'd do that? Deliberately refuse to help someone who was drowning?" He glared at Mark, challenging him with hard eyes and a menacing tone. Secretly, he was glad to see that Mark was not going to back down without a fight, like so many others did.

On the contrary, Mark took a step closer, glaring down into Jack's face. "I don't know what you would do. I only know you were out there in the gulf that day, a boat was overturned, a man was drowning, a woman screamed for your help. She could have died too!"

The horror of that possibility gave Mark the energy he needed to face the man down, although his words were spoken in a low yet firm tone of voice.

Jack tilted his head back, glaring into the condemning face above him. "Who told you this?" His eyes were narrowed suspiciously.

"She did."

Jack's eyes flared. "Ah, she did," Jack shook his head slowly, then headed for his bourbon. He no longer cared what Mark thought about his drinking. "She told you what a monster I am, no doubt, just as she told her lawyer. Now they're threatening to sue."

He grabbed a glass, tilted the decanter of bourbon, omitting the ice.

"You'd better learn something fast or you'll be whipped like a puppy before you ever start." He slugged down a drink of bourbon and froze, enduring the pain of its descent. He felt a spark of satisfaction at not coughing his head off in payment for the drink. "They're all out to get you, once they think they've got a leg to stand on. Most don't even have that. Money is fresh meat to vultures, and they're everywhere, all those little people who can't make it on their own and have to prey on people who have spent their lives — "

"Spent their lives dishonestly," Mark lashed back. "I've read the fine print in those contracts. I've seen how you take advantage of people who need loans."

Jack gripped the back of a barstool, anger mixing with the alcohol in his blood as he raised his voice and leveled his attack. He no longer cared that this was his son. Nobody was going to talk to him as this man had.

"So now that you've inherited it all, you're ready to tell me everything that's wrong with me and my company! You're going to flaunt your morals in my face and tell me what a louse I am!"

He finished the drink and slammed it down on the bar.

"Your money has nothing to do with this," Mark retaliated. "And if you don't believe me, I'm willing to call in the attorneys this minute. We'll reverse everything!"

Jack whirled and they glared at one another for several seconds as the standoff lengthened. Then Jack sank to the barstool, staring at the empty glass, saying nothing. To his utter amazement, he believed the fool boy meant it. Was he that bullheaded? he wondered. Or that honorable?

Honor was a word that scarcely touched his mind, or his vocabulary, but now he pondered it.

As he did, Mark stared at Jack, watching the flush of anger fade; his skin turned ashen once again. He looked terrible.

Mark's eyes moved from the man to the walls around them. He stared at all the trophies of Jack's adult years and wondered if the man had ever known happiness or even joy.

Mark's anger had drained into the silence. He was still consumed with frustration over Jessica, and all that had happened to her. Still, he felt his calm returning as he walked over to the bar and took a seat. He folded his hands on the bar and studied his fingers.

"This isn't about you and me," he said quietly. "I met a

woman here, a woman I like more than anyone I've ever met."

Jack's head snapped back, as he struggled to switch gears, follow this sudden turn in the mental war that waged between them.

"I had been seeing her," Mark continued, "while I tried to make a decision about staying here or returning to Birmingham. She goes by her maiden name, Thorne. She had told me in the beginning that she was married for less than a year when her husband died in a boating accident."

Jack cocked his head and peered through his thick lenses to Mark's face. He now realized where the conversation was going.

"Yesterday, over lunch, I learned that her married name was Vandercamp. And that she blames Jack Barkley more than anyone for her husband's death."

Jack slumped against the bar and stared at the tormented face of the young man before him. It was clear to him what had happened to Mark. Passion did that at first; it blinded a man to the truth. Looking into Mark's green eyes, he saw Paulette again, and his memory was swept back to that reckless time in his life when he had lost his heart, along with his common sense.

Paulette...

His eyes drifted over Mark's head. For several seconds he could see in his mind's eye the stunningly beautiful woman who had stolen his heart. He remembered the satin-smooth skin, the taunting look in those green eyes, the luscious red lips. She had rushed through his blood like a drug, and for a while he was hopelessly addicted.

He took a slow breath and focused again on the young

man seated before him, looking as miserable as Jack had felt the day Paulette walked out of his life. Forever.

Jack turned to contemplate his empty glass. He didn't want another drink, not now; he was too overcome with… something. And it had to do with the tenderness that filled his heart as he looked at Mark and understood what motivated him. It occurred to Jack, first and foremost, that he did not want to lose his son. He loved him! The word still astounded him, but it was true.

So what should he do? As always, his basic need to rule and control took over, and he tried to analyze the best way to win this game, regain the control he had lost.

"Mark, you have to believe me. I wouldn't just let somebody drown." Jack forced his mind back to the day, trying to remember everything. It had been a close call for him, as well.

"What happened?" Mark's voice was flat and cold.

Jack could tolerate Mark's tone, he wouldn't take offense now. He knew the enemy he was dealing with here. Passion for a woman.

"I woke up with pains in my chest that morning," Jack spoke slowly. "I thought it was too many cigars and the effects of a late-night poker game. Decided some sea air would help." He took a deep breath, trying his best to remember, though his brain had been clouded by a hangover. "A storm came up quick, the water got choppy in a hurry."

He leveled his gaze to Mark, facing him head-on with the bottom line. "You know I have a chauffeur. I don't drive anymore, don't take the boat out. On that day I went out alone. I shouldn't have. I have a cataract over my left eye. I'm legally blind. My doctor will confirm it. I get by with my right eye but my vision has become worse the past year. Naturally, I don't broadcast that fact. There are too many people ready to take advantage of me, once they see an opportunity."

His hand fumbled along the counter, fighting the urge for a good cigar. "When the storm came in, I knew I had to get to shore. And yes, I saw the overturned boat but it was a blur. I didn't see anyone in the water, but over the wind I thought I heard voices. I radioed the coast guard and went on."

For several seconds afterwards, there was complete silence in the room. Then Jack delivered the clincher.

"If you ask her who saved her, I'm sure she'll say it was the coast guard. And if I hadn't called them, she would have drowned too."

Fifteen

Jessica found the note on her door when she returned. She read it quickly, trying not to feel anything for Mark Castleman. He had hurt her deeply, and now he was the catalyst for a fight with her in-laws. She felt terrible about that.

Wadding the note, she unlocked the door and entered the still house. Wilma was spending this Sunday with friends and wouldn't be home until evening, but for once she was glad not to face Wilma's pleasant smile. She needed to be alone.

She walked stiffly to the kitchen, hoping that some strong tea would ease the ache in her body. She wished there was something she could do for her mind. Suddenly she remembered a Scripture verse from childhood, a verse she had mentally repeated like a litany that day in the water when she feared she would drown.

"The Lord is my shepherd…" What was the rest of it? "…I will fear no evil, for thou art with me…"

The tears came again and she sank to the kitchen chair.

Maybe if she had kept reading those Scriptures, stayed in church, she would have been wiser about Blake, about everything else that had happened to her. Well, there was no going back; she had to go forward, although she didn't know how.

Her eyes fell to the newspaper again and she could see a few damp traces where her tears had dripped onto the print. She looked away, unwilling to see his picture or read the caption again. She was aware of the crumpled note in her palm and now she tossed it into the wastebasket.

What was she going to do? She had alienated Sue and Mel, and they were her last hope for financial help. If they didn't come through for her, she would be forced to give up Seascape. She placed little faith in that application she had left at the bank.

Her mind screamed a dozen desperate reminders…the hard work, the long hours, the dreams, the hopes, the plans….

The kettle began to sing and she dragged herself out of the chair. Dropping a tea bag in a cup, she poured steaming water from the kettle. She had to get through today, and that was taking every ounce of strength. She considered calling her parents, but she remembered that her mom was getting over the flu and her dad was traveling.

No, she wouldn't call, for she knew what would happen. Mom would beg her to come back to Louisville to live, as she had done when Blake died. But Jessica hadn't wanted to return to Louisville, or her parents' home for that matter. Just one more act of defiance on her part. Or disobedience. Which was it?

She closed her eyes waiting for the tea to steep. Had she

been subconsciously punishing her parents for all the moves during her growing-up years? She had resented having to pick up and move every time she made new friends.

A weary sigh shook her as she removed the tea bag and laid it on a napkin. Well, she'd like to tell all women considering marriage to listen to their parents. Not only had she hurt them, she had hurt herself even more.

What was she going to do? How was she going to operate Seascape and pay her bills?

She sat sipping her tea as her eyes drifted over the kitchen. She had come to feel a real sense of home here, her first real home since leaving Angel Valley. Surveying the cabinets she had painted, the walls she had papered, she thought of the countless hours she had invested here. In the process, she had learned a lot about herself. She was strong, much stronger than she ever knew. She'd find a way to hang on to Seascape.

Doris, Jack's housekeeper, had prepared an early dinner for Mark and Jack, and now they sat at the table, eating in silence. Mark was drained by the emotion that had racked him all day, and Jack was ill, though he tried to conceal it.

At last Mark focused on him and leaned back in the chair. "I know you don't believe in God, but —"

"I never said that," Jack barked, then calmed himself. He reached for a roll, then held it in his hand for a moment, staring at it. "My mother was religious," he said faintly, "but she died when I was young."

Mark looked across the gleaming cherrywood table to Jack. He owed this man the only gift he could give him and he must do it now, before it was too late. "Excuse me, I want to get something out of the car."

Mark left the room with Jack staring after him, hearing the front door close. *What's he up to now?* Jack wondered. Mark was a source of endless fascination to him. He found it almost impossible to believe that his own blood ran through the veins of this remarkable young man.

Again his eyes felt strange, moist! He cursed himself for turning into a sissy in his last days, and he quickly dropped his eyes to his food as the front door closed again and Mark returned to the room.

"Here, I want you to have these," Mark said.

Jack squinted at the items in Mark's hand. "What are they?" he muttered. No one ever gave him anything, so he looked and sounded awkward in accepting a gift.

"Audio tapes of the New Testament. You can listen to the tapes at night when you go to bed. I noticed you have a tape player as part of the radio in the kitchen."

Jack stared at the tapes Mark placed beside him.

"Mom gave them to me as I was leaving. I had complained about the long drive; she said I could listen to something worthwhile as I traveled."

Avoiding Mark's eyes, Jack stared at the audio tapes. "She must be a nice woman," he said hoarsely.

"She's a wonderful woman." Mark took his seat again. "Maybe you'll get to meet her."

Jack said nothing, but he doubted he would last long enough to meet the people who had raised Mark. He didn't want to meet the man Mark called Dad. The woman? Maybe he would like to meet her.

"Jack?"

At the sound of Mark's voice, Jack's head shot up. There was gentleness in his tone, which amazed Jack, considering what Jack had learned about this woman, Jessica.

With pain-filled eyes, Jack looked at the young man he was coming to love so much. It was easy to love Mark; even if he wasn't his son, Jack knew he would be impressed with him. And he didn't like many people.

"Look...," Mark hesitated, choosing his words carefully. "I was raised by Christian people who taught me there is a God who cares about me, about everyone, and that no matter what I've done he's willing to forgive." As he looked Jack straight in the eye, Mark wondered if anyone other than Jack's mother had talked to him about God. "I wish you'd listen to those tapes."

Mark took a deep breath, not wanting to push too hard. He was amazed that a man like Jack had let him get this far.

Jack said nothing. He merely stared at Mark for several seconds after he finished speaking.

Doris appeared at the table, offering dessert. Both men refused, but Mark couldn't help noticing that Jack spoke more kindly to her than he had earlier.

After dinner, they returned to the den to watch a news show Jack always watched on Sunday evenings. Mark decided to stay on. He had noticed a definite change in the man, just since Friday. His breathing was labored, his color was terrible. He considered telling Jack he knew about his condition, but he had promised Walter to keep quiet. And, too, Jack would think he was only hanging around, waiting for him to die. This was not true, but it was the way Jack's mind worked. Motives. Jack figured everyone had a motive for their actions.

Later, glancing at Jack, slumped in his recliner, his face ashen, Mark knew Walter had told him the truth. He doubted he would last three months, or perhaps even a month.

His mind wandered back to Jessica. Would he ever be able to make her understand his situation? Would he ever get the chance? Mark sighed. Not likely. There was only one thing to do. He simply had to forget about her.

It was late when Mark decided to leave. Jack had been dozing in his recliner off and on for the past hour. Finally, Mark stood and stretched, looking down at the end table beside Jack's recliner. There sat the tapes Mark had given him. Jack had picked them up from the table and brought them with him. But would he ever listen to them?

After hearing about Jack's failing eyesight, Mark knew the man needed those tapes more than anything else he could give him.

Mark stared at Jack, oddly stirred by feelings he couldn't yet define; nor was he ready to confront those feelings. He crossed the room and touched Jack lightly on the shoulder.

Jack's eyes dragged open. "I'm leaving now," Mark said. "You'd better go to bed." Mark remembered he had planned to leave for Alabama after church today. That was before he picked up the morning paper.

He took a deep breath, trying to clear his thoughts. "I need to go to Birmingham in the morning. I have to pick up more clothes and arrange to have my furniture sent down here."

Jack nodded. "Do what you have to."

"I'll be back in a day or two." He hesitated. "Take care of yourself."

On the drive home, he thought about calling Jessica one more time, even though he had decided the wisest course of action was to try to forget her. It would be easier for both of them. He just hated for her to think he was such a liar.

He weighed the pros and cons of trying one more time to speak with her during his half-hour drive to the beach. By the time he reached his condo and unlocked the door, he had decided to make one last effort. He had nothing to lose. Maybe after reading the note, she wouldn't hang up this time.

He hurried to the phone while he still had the courage. Lifting the receiver, he dialed and waited as the number began to ring. He had never been so nervous over a phone call to a woman, not even his first phone call in junior high to Betsy Rutherford. After four rings, he decided that maybe she had gone to Louisville, after all.

The sound of her voice struck a blow in his heart, but he reminded himself of the reason he had called.

"Jessica, don't hang up. Just listen for a minute —"

"No, you listen! If you ever come to my house again, or call me or try to see me, I'll get a restraining order. And I mean that."

The phone clicked in his ear. He held it for a few seconds staring into space, then with a sigh he hung up. This settled it. He had done all he could. He would never try to see her or speak with her again.

Jessica glared at the phone, his voice still echoing in her ear, haunting her. She took a deep breath and closed her eyes, trying to shut out the pleading quality she had heard in that voice. For a split second, she had almost relented. Then, with the force of a tidal wave, all the anger and hate rushed back, saving her. Boy, was she ever a sucker for a story, any story. First Blake, now Mark, and the sad thing was she had almost listened to Mark, almost. Her weakness terrified her.

Wilma poked her head in the door, and for the first time, Jessica found herself resenting the older woman's good intentions.

"Was that him?" Wilma asked.

Jessica nodded stiffly. Wilma had come home and found her crying, and Jessica had told her everything. "Yes, that was him," she sighed, switching off the overhead light and turning on the night-light over the sink.

"Maybe you should hear him out," Wilma suggested.

"No! And if you don't mind, I'll tend to this myself." She bit her lip. "Wilma, I'm sorry. I didn't mean to bite your head off. As you can see, the pressure is getting to me."

"And it's no wonder!" Wilma was shaking her head, looking Jessica up and down. "You've had more than your share of trouble, bless your heart."

"Well, I blame myself for some of this," Jessica sighed.

"Blame yourself? Oh, but you mustn't do that. None of this is your fault."

Jessica swallowed, staring at the floor. "My father-in-law thinks I sold out to Barkley by accepting an extension on my mortgage payments. Now, after the way…" She could not bring herself to speak Mark's name, "after the way Barkley's son deceived me, I wish I had gone on with the lawsuit."

Wilma pursed her lips, studying her. "It isn't too late just because that McCormick fellow didn't help you. There are plenty of other attorneys. My friend, Anna Williamson, brought a lawsuit against a big hotel here. Anna tripped over a loose step, fell, and broke her hip. She was in the hospital for weeks. Fortunately, she had a good attorney who didn't back down to those fancy hotel executives."

Jessica looked at her curiously. "Who was her attorney?"

Wilma frowned. "I don't remember. Why don't I get the name for you, and you could go talk with him?"

Jessica stared at Wilma for a moment, considering the idea. Then slowly she began to nod. "Why not?"

Sixteen

Monday was turning out to be a good day, Jessica decided, as she left the office of her new attorney. Passing the secretary's desk, Jessica interrupted a personal conversation between the secretary and a man who must be her boyfriend, judging from the looks passing back and forth between them.

"Excuse me," Jessica said, "but I need to schedule another appointment. And Mr. Jacobson asked me to leave these papers with you."

Jessica was holding her mortgage papers, along with the picture of Mark and Jack from Sunday's newspaper.

As the secretary flipped through the appointment book, Jessica was conscious of the secretary's boyfriend staring at the picture in the paper. Once she had an appointment, Jessica headed for the elevator and punched the button.

When the doors slid open and she stepped on, she noticed the man was right behind her. She pushed a button for the lobby and glanced at him.

"Same for me," he said with a pleasant smile.

She pressed the button and leaned back against the wall, waiting as the elevator began its descent.

"Excuse me," he spoke up, "but I couldn't help noticing the clipping you gave Erin. I happen to work for the other paper." He grinned. "We're just the little guys."

She arched an eyebrow. "I know what you mean." She was unable to keep the cynicism from her tone, not that it mattered.

"Did you…that is…" he cleared his throat and plunged on. "You're obviously at the attorney's office for a reason. Has the Barkley Corporation done something to you?"

She looked at him sharply, tempted to ask what business it was of his. Then she shrugged. Why not tell him and all the world as well? It was the quickest way she'd get any revenge.

"As a matter of fact, I blame Jack Barkley for the death of my husband."

He lurched forward, unable to control himself. "You don't say?"

The elevator doors slid open and Jessica stepped off with the reporter hot on her heels.

"Look, could we have a cup of coffee and talk?" he asked. "You're one of the few people willing to speak out against Barkley. I personally think that company is crooked and disreputable. Other people think so too, but nobody will say anything."

Jessica stopped walking and turned to face the guy who stood beside her, whipping out a business card. She could see a small notebook and a pen in the pocket of his jacket. So he was a newspaper reporter. If she wanted revenge, here was her chance.

"I'm not afraid to say what I think of Jack Barkley…or his son, for that matter." A slow smile began to form on her lips as she glanced toward the adjoining coffee shop. "Sure, I'll have coffee with you."

Jack had slept well for the first time in months. The tape had poured words into his tormented brain that soothed and comforted him. How strange that words from a tape could do that; no, not just words, he corrected himself. He had listened to a story he hadn't heard since childhood, a story told through Scriptures. It was about a God who gave his Son to die for the sins of the world.

The story kept haunting him; in fact, he was tempted to stay home and listen to more tapes. He was fascinated in a way he could neither understand nor explain.

He sat at the breakfast table, thinking about Mark and the tapes. Then his mind wandered to the woman, Jessica. Mark cared for her. More than anyone he had ever met, he had told Jack.

Jack sighed heavily and dawdled over his coffee, fully aware he should be getting dressed. The chauffeur would be along soon, but let him wait. He was being paid well; he shouldn't mind sitting in the driveway, listening to that rock music of his.

Doris slipped in to refill his coffee cup. "Want more toast, Mr. Barkley?" she asked as softly as possible.

"No, thank you, Doris."

She almost dropped the pot at his kind tone of voice. She stared at him, thinking about the picture in yesterday's paper. Maybe Mr. Barkley was relieved to have his son take over the company. She smiled to herself and returned to the kitchen where she could ponder his change of mood over a second cup of coffee.

Jack removed his glasses and rubbed his eyes, thinking again of that awful day he had been caught in the storm out on the water. He had told Mark the truth. The sight of an overturned boat had blurred before him that day with the ocean spraying in his face and the terror of his own circumstances overpowering the needs of others. Young fools who should have been able to fend for themselves; at least, they could see clearly.

Still, if he could have saved a man's life.... He dropped his head, wondering if there was any way he could make amends to this woman. He knew the company had financed her house at the beach, that much was clear to him after his chief attorney told him he'd struck a deal with McCormick to allow her to catch up.

Catch up. His mind seemed so muddled these days. He felt as though he were stumbling around in a fog of confusion. It was more difficult with each day, and particularly now, with the medicine.

Catch up...

The words lingered in his mind as he reached for the mobile phone nearby. He dialed Walter's private line and found him at his desk, just as he expected. He reminded himself to change his will, give Walter more shares, and some cash as well.

"Walter, I want you to pull the mortgage we're carrying on Vandercamp."

He hesitated, waiting for a rush of anxious words from Walter.

"Vandercamp. The woman who's threatening to sue?"

"Yes, that's the one. Mark the account paid in full and send her the deed."

Walter began sputtering objections, but Jack cut him off. "Just do it, Walter. And by the way, I don't think I'm coming in today."

He hung up, sighing with relief. As he sat thinking about what he had done, a feeling of peace slipped over him. He pulled himself up from the table, thinking again about the tapes.

Mark had been on the road for two hours when Jack made the phone call that would change Jessica's life. If Mark had known about Jack's act of kindness, he would have been surprised and pleased. But he did not and he drove along staring at the interstate, feeling an ache of sadness as he thought about Jessica.

At that same hour, Jessica awoke with a headache and a sense of foreboding. She sat up in bed, rubbed her eyes, and glanced at the clock. It was after eight and she had overslept. She could already hear Wilma puttering around in the kitchen. Hugging her knees to her chest, she stared into space, thinking about her interview with the reporter.

They had sat in the coffee shop for over an hour while he furiously jotted notes. She had wanted to talk, needed to talk, but as soon as she arrived home, pinpoints of regret began to prick her conscience. She had tried to ignore the little whispers in her brain, but now those whispers were growing louder and her conscience was nagging again.

She got out of bed and reached for her robe, forgoing the usual routine of a shower and shampoo until later as she wandered into the kitchen and sank into a chair.

Wilma was already seated at the table, sipping tea and staring into space.

"Where's the smile, Wilma?" Jessica asked, making a wry attempt at humor.

"Robin's letter took it away." Wilma shook her head, staring at the pages unfolded on the table. "I don't know what to do about that girl, Jessica."

"What's wrong?" Jessica asked, concerned to see that her friend was so worried.

"Well...," she pushed the letter aside and picked up the snapshot that had been enclosed.

"May I see?" Jessica asked, taking a seat at the table.

Wilma handed her the picture. "Took after her father's side of the family."

"She's very pretty," Jessica said, studying the picture.

A mass of strawberry blond hair framed a square jaw, uptilted nose, and full mouth. She wore a denim shorts suit with a bright red T-shirt underneath. Huge silver hoops dangled from her ears, and a matching silver bracelet circled her right arm. She appeared to be tall with long legs that looked well-toned above hiking boots.

"Yes, she is," Wilma sighed, "but she's such an adventurer." A weary smile touched her lips as Jessica returned the picture and Wilma stared at her daughter for a few seconds. "She likes to say she enjoys life and people and wants to cram in as much of that enjoyment as possible. But she traipses all over the country, from one job to another. Now she wants to spend the summer out in the wilds of British Columbia. She's always been curious about her ancestors who homesteaded a ranch out in grizzly country."

Jessica reached across, touching Wilma's hand. "Don't worry, Wilma. She's only talking about a summer, and it will be an interesting adventure for her." Hearing herself speak those words recalled her own misguided adventures the past year. She slumped deeper in her chair.

"Looks as though you need a bracing cup of tea as well," Wilma said, getting up for the teapot and a cup.

"Thanks," Jessica forced a weak smile and studied the kind woman who seemed to reflect a peace amid life's storms. "Wilma, have you ever done anything on the spur of the moment, then hated yourself later?"

Wilma laughed. "Hasn't everyone?"

Jessica shrugged. "I suppose."

"Are you worried about that interview?"

Jessica pressed her fingers to her throbbing temples. "I regret that I didn't take longer to think about what I was saying." She sighed, took a sip of tea, then continued. "You know how I feel about Barkley and his son, but still...." She shook her head and the pain accelerated. "It's just never been my nature to retaliate as I did yesterday. I don't know what's happening to me." She felt the sting of tears before she dropped her eyes.

Wilma patted her arm. "Remind me to tell you the story of Eugenia, my grandmother. This is the grandmother who fascinates Robin so much. As a bride, Granny Russell followed her husband to the heart of the wilderness and spent her life helping him tame that raw country. My mother was the youngest of four children. She married young and moved over to Cranbrook, but I grew up hearing stories of hardship and courage from her pioneer days. I always thought my grandmother was the bravest person I ever heard about. Until I met you."

Jessica raised dreary eyes to Wilma. "I don't feel very brave at the moment."

Wilma's blue eyes twinkled at the edges as she smiled at Jessica. "You're doing the best you can under very difficult circumstances. Allow yourself a few mistakes, Jessica. We're only human."

Jessica nodded. "I know, but my conscience is bothering me, Wilma. And I'm not sure why."

"When will the interview be published?"

"Soon, I think." Jessica raised her eyes to the window and studied the sunshine on the windowsill. "Maybe I'll call that reporter. After my conference with the attorney yesterday, I was fuming over the Barkleys.

Wilma nodded. She could understand that. "Why don't you take the day to think things over? See how you feel this afternoon. If you're still apprehensive, you might be wise to postpone the story until you're sure about your feelings."

Jessica took a deep breath, glancing across at Wilma. She tried to smile. "That sounds like a good idea. Thanks, Wilma." She kept thinking about Mark, hating herself each time she allowed his memory to cross her mind. Yet, she couldn't seem to keep him locked out. Her eyes darkened and another wave of depression threatened to hit.

Maybe romance works out for some people, but not me, she thought grimly. A husband obviously wasn't in the plan for her life. She had been so sure of Mark, and now her judgment had failed her again.

Pushing back from the table, she stood and faced Wilma with a determined set to her chin.

"I'm going to scrub the floors today. I need to get rid of some frustration, and attacking these floors is the best way I can think of to do that."

Wilma thought the floors looked fine, but she wasn't about to argue with Jessica. She knew her young friend needed to stay busy. As for the house, she had watched Jessica pour her heart and soul into the place; she only hoped it paid off for her.

Late in the afternoon, aching from head to toe, Jessica stepped into the shower and let the spray pelt her sore muscles. She had mopped and waxed every floor and swept the porches a second time.

Wilma tried to help, then wisely gave up and went to her room for a nap.

As Jessica stood under the shower head, enjoying the feel and smell of the special soap that Laurel had sent her, her thoughts drifted to Angel Valley. Maybe she'd take a couple days off and drive up there, make arrangements to buy those rockers. She knew Clarence would let her pay later; he was wonderful about that. Yes, she decided, reaching for the shampoo, a quick trip to the mountains was exactly what she needed.

When finally head and body were squeaky clean, she stepped out of the shower, toweled down and reached for her robe. After thinking the matter over throughout the day, she had decided to call the reporter and ask to read his article before it was printed.

She walked into the bedroom and retrieved his business card from her purse. Pushing the turbaned towel higher on her head, she dialed his number. When he answered she explained why she had called and waited for him to respond. Several seconds passed before he did.

A heavy sigh filled the wire. "It's too late. My story has already gone to press. It will be in tomorrow's paper."

"Oh." Jessica gripped the phone, staring at his name on the card. "It's just that…well, I was worried that I may have come across too harsh."

"You just told the truth, didn't you?"

"Of course I did."

"And I reported what you told me. Don't worry. I think a lot of people are going to benefit from this story. There's one thing for sure: Barkley won't be so quick to bully other people now that somebody has finally called his hand."

Jessica chewed the inside of her lip. "I hope so."

She hung up, as troubled as she had been at breakfast, in spite of the reporter's attempts to convince her that she had done the right thing.

Absently, she lifted a hand and removed the towel and began to dry her hair. Had she done the right thing?

That question was answered sooner than she expected when her new attorney called the next day.

"Jessica, this is Claude Jacobson. You should never have done that interview," he snapped.

"Why not?" she replied tartly, trying to bluff her way through this.

"Because you don't pull a stunt like that before we're ready. Another thing, we may have trouble proving Barkley saw you that day. I've learned he has a problem with his vision. If that's true, he may file suit against you for slander."

Jessica was horrified at those words. "That man's problem

is not with his vision, but with his heart. He's never used it."

After a few more biting words, Jacobson hung up. Jessica grabbed her car keys and ran out to her car. All she could think about was how her words came across in the story. Already, she was feeling sick with dread. And regret. She found a newsstand at the grocery several blocks away, wheeled to the curb and left the car running.

She found the story right away. The opening sentence grabbed one's attention with the news of a lawsuit filed by Jessica Thorne Vandercamp, wife of deceased Blake Vandercamp, against J. C. Barkley. In a clear and concise manner, the reporter repeated her words accurately. The mortgage on her home was mentioned, along with the fact that Mark Castleman, Barkley's son, had misrepresented himself to her in an effort to win her affections and by doing so ward off a lawsuit against his father.

When Jessica finished reading, she stared into space and tried to consider the story objectively. He had quoted her accurately, and yet she was not happy with the story or with herself.

She got in the car and drove home, wondering what the Barkleys would think.

Jack saw the paper before Mark did. Walter had arrived in the late afternoon, expecting to find Jack at the bar. To his surprise, he was seated out on the patio, his hands folded in his lap, listening to an audio tape.

Walter came up short, gawking at him. He had done as instructed about the mortgage on the woman's house; the paperwork was already being processed. Seeing the paper had thrown Walter into shock, however, and he couldn't imagine what this was going to do to Jack. At the office, the phones were already ringing off the hook with reporters wanting opinions, quotes, even a story to counter her claims.

All these things were running through Walter's mind as he stood staring at Jack. He cleared his throat. "Jack?"

Slowly, Jack turned to face him, motioning him to a chair as he turned off the tape player. Walter stared at the machine, having heard enough words to absolutely stun him. It had sounded like some sort of Bible stuff, and he wondered if Jack's mind had finally snapped under all the pressure.

"Want some coffee, Walter?" Jack asked, squinting at him.

"Jack, we've got a big problem," he burst out, skipping the preliminaries. "That Vandercamp woman is suing us after all. And telling the world about it." He thrust the newspaper in Jack's hands.

For several seconds, Jack didn't appear to register the information he had been given. Then slowly he fumbled for the glasses he had removed earlier and left on the table beside the recorder. Jack put on his glasses and lifted the paper close to his face, frowning. Then he laid it in his lap and turned to Walter. "Just tell me what it says."

Walter went over the story, practically word for word, and waited for the explosion. It didn't come.

Jack pressed his head back against the cushioned chair and stared into space for a moment, saying nothing.

"The girl has spirit, doesn't she?" he finally replied.

Walter's mouth fell open. Now he was certain the old man's mind had snapped. Walter fidgeted, trying to think what to do. He would consult the hotshot young CEO. Let Mark handle this one!

"Where's Mark?" he asked, frowning.

"Drove up to Birmingham to move the rest of his belongings down here." Jack yawned. "I'm proud of him, Walter."

"Jack." Walter grabbed a breath and tried to choose his words. His nerves were as taut as a tightrope, while his mind struggled with a balancing act. He wanted to emphasize to Jack the seriousness of this lawsuit, particularly after the story, and yet he felt he needed to cushion him from further shock. He cleared his throat and began again. "We may be in serious trouble with this story, Jack," he said in low measured tones.

Jack rolled his head and fixed Walter with a dull stare. "We've been in serious trouble before, Walter. She's right, though. I could have saved his life and I didn't."

Walter couldn't suppress his gasp of shock. "Jack," he said hoarsely, "I know you're sensitive about your eyes, but I'm aware of how poor your vision is. I always figured you didn't really see that guy out there in the water."

Jack heaved a sigh. "I didn't see him. But if I had, I might not have cared at that time. Walter, I've been a lousy human being, I've lived a terrible life."

To Walter's utter amazement, tears were rolling down the face of the man he had always thought incapable of tears. He tried desperately to find the right words to say but failed. He decided the best thing he could do was turn away from Jack, spare him the anguish of having someone witness his emotion.

Walter leapt out of his chair and lurched toward the patio rail, pretending an interest in the sky. From behind him, he could hear a snort, and then it sounded as though Jack was blowing his nose.

"I'll cancel the paperwork on that woman's mortgage," Walter called gruffly. "She's got her nerve —"

"Let it alone. Send her the deed, as I instructed."

He whirled. "You're not serious."

"Yes, I am." Jack came to his feet, rather unsteadily. "Walter, I'm going to bed."

Walter was staring at Jack's red eyes. "What do you want to do about that story, Jack? And a lawsuit —"

"Nothing. I don't want to do anything about it." He turned and trudged out of the room.

Walter stared after him, a multitude of thoughts hurtling through his confused brain. Foremost was the knowledge that he had never seen Jack walk so slow or look so frail. And yet there was a peace about him, a human side that Walter had never seen. His eyes fell to the tape player, and he leaned down, peering at the title of the tapes.

The New Testament.

He wondered how many more shocks he could take before he became as addled as Jack. Striding back through the den to Jack's personal office, he found Mark's Birmingham number scrawled on a pad and quickly dialed it.

The fact that he had caught up with Mark was the first piece of good luck Walter had all day, and he heaved a sigh at the sound of his voice.

"Mark, it's Walter," he said breathlessly. "We've got a big problem here."

"Walter? Is Jack worse?" Mark asked.

Mark stood in the den of his parents' home clutching the desk phone. He had been about to join his parents for dinner when the phone rang.

"Jack's not well at all," Walter confirmed. His eyes shot

toward the open door. He had a glimpse of Jack's lounging robe as he climbed the steps to his bedroom. "But that's not the main reason I called."

He launched into the disastrous story. He finished with the news that he had told Jack about the story, and that Jack didn't seem to care.

"What are we going to do, Mark? This could be a disaster for the company."

Mark stared into space. He couldn't believe Jessica would do a thing like this; how could she? She must hate them both more than he had even imagined.

"I'll leave early in the morning," Mark said. He had wanted to spend more time with his parents. He felt he owed them that, but it now appeared he needed to get back to Florida as quickly as possible.

"Good, we need you. The other thing is, Jack's ordered me to mark her note paid in full and send her the deed. Isn't that crazy?"

Mark chewed his lip, thinking. He was angry with Jessica, really angry. Still, if Jack was being that generous, he was probably trying to make up for the past.

"No, I don't think it's crazy," Mark answered. "It may be the best way to ward off a lawsuit. And the cheapest. I think Jack is trying to salve his conscience." Mark hated to do anything for her now, particularly since she had taken such a cheap shot at them. Still, his conscience told him it was the right thing to do. "Do it," he instructed Walter. "Then if she still wants a fight, we'll give her one. My conscience is clear."

Walter listened, thinking about what Mark had said, and he began to nod. Maybe the kid was right.

"Okay, see you tomorrow," Walter said, feeling better.

As he hung up, he began to appreciate the calm yet intelligent young man who was now CEO of the Barkley Corporation. Walter had assumed that Jack would still be running things, but it was obvious to him that Jack was in his final days.

In Birmingham, Mark stood holding the phone long after the wire had clicked. He had always been stubborn, but Jessica was about to find out just how stubborn he could be. He was not one for cheap shots, but he was angry at her now, really angry. She seemed to have forgotten that he had a law degree and he knew how to fight fire with fire.

Seventeen

When Jessica reached into her mailbox and pulled out the thick envelope from the Barkley Corporation, she cringed. Her attorney had phoned again to say it was quite likely that Barkley would file a suit against her for slander. What else could go wrong? she wondered, sinking down on the porch step to open the thick packet.

The cover letter was from the legal department, stating that J. C. Barkley had cancelled her debt in full. Her fingers trembled as she held the deed to the house and property, signed over to her.

For several moments, her brain refused to register what she held before her. Then she decided there had to be a trick to this, some legal maneuver designed to shut her up.

Shut her up, that was it! She got up and went inside the house and phoned her attorney, who was just as puzzled as Jessica upon hearing the news.

"Come in for a meeting first thing in the morning," he instructed her. "Bring everything."

"What do you make of this?" she asked, feeling light-headed from the possibility that she just might own the house, free and clear.

"Looks like you got your house back. But we may not be bought off that easily, right?"

She frowned, wondering. "I don't know what to think."

"See you at eight," he replied. "I'm late in court." He hung up, leaving her to wonder what on earth the Barkleys were up to now.

At dusk the next evening, Mark sat beside Jack's bed, staring down into his pale face. The blood seemed to have drained from his body, and his breathing was labored despite the oxygen. Jack had refused to go to the hospital, or have a doctor and nurse hovering over him. The doctor had come again this afternoon, given him a shot, and left, and Jack had been asleep for the past hour.

Mark sat in the luxurious bedroom, his legs stretched out, his eyes fixed on Jack. He was thinking about what an empty, lonely life the man had lived. Many associates had called to check on him, but only Walter, Doris, and one other executive from the company showed any real concern. Mark thought it was the saddest thing he had ever witnessed, the passing of a wasted life.

Jack's eyes fluttered open and tried to focus on Mark.

"Hey, I'm here," Mark said, leaning toward the bed.

"Mark…the tapes…" Jack's voice was no more than a rasp in the still room, and a weak one at that.

"I'm glad you listened to the tapes," Mark said, trying to speak for him. Mark had found the tapes and the machine earlier and was pleased to see the last tape in the series was on the machine.

"I want to…make my life…right…before —"

Mark nodded, understanding what Jack wanted to say. "Shall I call a minister?"

Jack's head rolled slowly against the crisp white pillow. "You're…the best minister…I ever met."

The sound of Jack's ragged breath warned Mark that time was running out. He thought about the words a minister had spoken to him as a teenager when he gave his heart to God. Gripping Jack's lifeless hand, Mark tried to keep the message simple.

"Jack, what you need to do is pray a prayer with me. A minister would call it a sinner's prayer. You just ask God to come into your heart and forgive your sins. And you need to believe that he sent his Son to die on the cross. Can you do that?"

Jack nodded.

Mark gripped his hand tighter. "Then pray with me now.…"

Jessica had arrived at the attorney's office promptly at eight. She glanced cautiously around the hall and reception area, worried that the newspaper reporter would be waiting. He was nowhere in sight.

The secretary ushered her into the attorney's office, and as soon as he saw Jessica, he came to his feet, frowning.

"Have you heard?" he asked in greeting her.

Looking at his grim face, she suspected there had been another turn of events in her drama with the Barkleys. She tried to steel herself for the news of a counter-suit.

"Heard what?" she asked flatly.

"Jack Barkley died last night. Lung cancer."

Jessica stared at the attorney, stunned for a moment. Then she began thinking of Mark.

The attorney sank into his seat and motioned her to a chair. "Apparently, he's been ill for some time." He drummed his fingers on the papers before him as both thought about this news for a full minute. "What do you want to do?" he asked, his eyes sweeping her.

She leaned back in the chair, her mind spinning. "Why do you think he cancelled the debt?"

He shrugged. "If he knew he was dying, maybe it was a way of making amends. We can still go after the estate for damages."

She closed her eyes, hating the sound of those words. Suddenly she remembered the newspaper story two days before, and she couldn't help wondering what the bad publicity had done to him. She opened her eyes and took a deep breath.

"No. Maybe I already have my revenge. And I'll tell you something, Mr. Jacobson, I don't like the way it feels. I don't like it at all."

She had left his office before she gave way to the emotion that welled inside of her. She was disgusted with attorneys, disgusted with lawsuits, and she was quite disgusted with herself.

No matter how conniving Barkley and his son had been, she didn't like herself for stooping to their level. And now that he had cancelled her mortgage, she felt a knot of emotions that was difficult to untangle.

When she arrived back home and turned in to the drive, she spotted the Vandercamps' van parked in the driveway. Mel and Sue sat on the porch talking to one another.

"I'm not up to this," she mumbled under her breath, trying to summon her failing strength.

Slowly, she got out of her car, remembering her recent argument with them. The last thing she wanted to do was fight with Sue and Mel; it was too difficult for everyone concerned. Maybe they were here to patch things up. She wanted to do that too.

They were on their feet, waiting, as she approached the porch.

"Hello, dear," Sue rushed forward, throwing her small arms around Jessica as though nothing had happened.

"Place is looking good," Mel called pleasantly.

"Thanks. I'm proud of it," she said, as they all turned to survey the outside of the house. She had expected Mel to complain about the color, but he didn't. He even told her he was impressed with what she had done. Jessica suspected that Sue had already warned him to be nice; she'd heard her do that in other situations.

"Come on inside," Jessica called, heading for the door.

"We can't stay," Sue replied. "We just wanted to pop by and say hello, see how you're doing."

Jessica turned back, glancing from Sue to Mel. "Well, two pretty startling things have happened. Barkley has cancelled my debt and returned the deed —"

"They're up to something," Mel barked, his mood already changing at the mention of the name Barkley.

"I've just come from the attorney's office," Jessica continued smoothly. "He looked everything over. It's perfectly legal. I now own the property free and clear."

Mel and Sue exchanged shocked glances. Then Mel wheeled on Jessica, abandoning his attempt to be polite. "You can't let it go at that. It's a setup to buy you off again."

Jessica's shoulders stiffened at the word "again." She looked at Sue, gauging her reaction. Sue was wringing her hands, looking from Mel to Jessica, then back to Mel.

"The other news is that Barkley died last night," Jessica said.

Obviously they had not heard that. Both sank into the porch chairs, staring at one another. The silence lengthened as Jessica waited for a reaction from them, then she decided to go on with what she was about to say.

"I'm going to drop the lawsuit."

"You can't do that!" Mel sprang from his chair. "You can still sue the estate and —"

"I'm not going to do that," she answered firmly. Her voice was low yet steady, and she looked him straight in the eye as she spoke.

Mel's eyes darkened. "So you're going to let them buy you off for — what?" He glanced back over his shoulder. "Fifty thousand? Is that what you owe?"

Jessica could no longer hold her tongue. "No, that isn't what I owe. Blake paid two hundred fifty thousand for this house!"

Both gasped; the color drained from Sue's face while Mel's frown deepened. "He wouldn't —"

"He did. Why would I lie to you?" She stopped herself before she went into the rest of it — the other debts, the extensive repairs, the money she had borrowed from her parents.

Mel had turned to Sue, his face dark with fury. "We'd better go."

Sue was staring at Jessica, trying to absorb everything she had heard. "So…how much is left owing on the house?"

"It doesn't matter," Mel thundered, stalking off. "It doesn't pay for Blake's life!"

His voice broke as his steps lengthened, and as Jessica watched him leave, she knew she could not tell him anything more. Let him believe she was being a coward; that would be easier than telling him the truth about his only child.

Sue's hand touched her arm. "Jessica, I know you've had a bad situation here. I think you've done a wonderful job, and I'm proud of you." Tears shimmered in Sue's eyes as she spoke.

Jessica forced a smile. "I'm sorry that he's upset. I tried to spare you…"

"I know. God bless you," she said, hugging her quickly before she dashed off to join her husband.

Jessica opened the door and walked into the living room, feeling as though she had just aged ten years. It was so draining emotionally to deal with them. Seeing their pain, she was glad she had not lost her temper. Still, she didn't know how many more confrontations she could take.

The house was quiet except for a slight movement overhead. She knew Wilma was up there, doing something helpful. Dusting, picking up, whatever. Strange that a perfect stranger had come into her life and helped her out far more than her in-laws.

She sighed, closing her eyes. There was no point in going over it anymore. The Vandercamps were the way they were and were too old to change. Perhaps they had always been blinded by their love for Blake, refusing to see his flaws, never disciplining him.

The sound of the van leaving the driveway faded in her ears, and she had a feeling she wouldn't be seeing much of them anymore. Maybe that was a good thing, for it was just too painful for all of them to sit and discuss Blake, or try to devise a scheme to make Barkley pay for what he had done.

She found her thoughts sneaking back to Mark again. Had he known Jack was dying? Lung cancer. That wasn't something that crept up overnight. Of course he had known. Perhaps that was why he had come here in the first place; it was obviously why he was taking over the corporation.

Still, there was no excuse for his deceit. The fact that he was taking over the company made that deceit even more unforgivable.

Well, she had not changed her mind about him. She never wanted to see him again. He was a schemer just like his father. She just wished she could keep him from creeping into her thoughts. And she wished she could stop trying to find reasons for what he had done. She had to get it through her thick skull, once and for all, that he was a cheat, just like Jack.

The word *cheat* just didn't fit. All her instincts about people argued with that conception of him. But then she reminded herself about her poor judgment. It had failed her with Blake and again with Mark. She had to accept that and go on.

Eighteen

Jessica read about the funeral in the paper as she sat alone on her porch, sipping at her tea, feeling utterly miserable. The newspaper account revealed that Jack Barkley had been in bad health for months, that he had died of lung cancer, survived by one son, Mark Castleman of Birmingham.

Birmingham. She leaned back against the chair and closed her eyes, thinking about Mark again. There had been some truth, then, in Mark's stories about Birmingham. Raised by his mother there, perhaps? No, he had mentioned a father. Probably a stepfather.

Her eyes dropped to the page again as she studied the small picture of Jack Barkley. He looked a bit different from the man she had seen in the boat. The man wore a sailor's hat and sunglasses, and he was much heavier. She tilted her head, staring at the picture. The thing that was most noticeable about this picture, and the other one announcing Mark's new position, was Barkley's thick-lensed glasses.

She recalled what her attorney had said. Barkley's legal staff claimed his vision was poor. Well, Jessica thought, that was their excuse. With glasses, he could still have seen them flailing in the ocean, begging for help. She wouldn't accept poor vision as an excuse. Nor would she allow herself to think of Mark Castleman ever again.

Laying the paper aside, she crossed her arms and looked down at the ocean, tossing and turning relentlessly beneath the March wind. What a strange year she had spent, and now she was about to begin a new career as owner of Seascape. Only a week away from tourist season, she had written personal letters to all her friends and family members, scattered across the country. She had done as much as she could to the house and was having to live on a shoe-string. But she would make it by being as economical as possible until the tourist money started coming in. Without the mortgage hanging over her head, she could survive.

The Vandercamps had kept their distance. This morning Sue had telephoned her and they had talked for a while. She had tried to be reassuring to Jessica, but then she had announced their intentions to return to Boston for a while. They couldn't take the summer heat here, and Mel had some business matters....

Jessica suspected they were merely making excuses to put some distance between themselves and Blake's widow, and a lot of bad memories.

Wilma had offered to grocery shop for her this morning, and Jessica had accepted. She needed to look over the brochure she had designed, advertising Seascape, before it went to the printer. With that in mind, she had turned to walk back inside when the sound of a car engine caught her attention.

An expensive-looking black car was parking in the driveway and now an attractive, middle-aged lady was getting out. Great! Her first customer.

Jessica hurried down the steps to greet her.

"Good morning," Jessica called with a smile.

"Good morning." The woman was tall with pale blonde hair, worn in a smooth pageboy, and friendly blue eyes. She looked to be in her late forties and was dressed fashionably in a white linen suit with gold jewelry. "How are you today?"

"Fine. And you?" Jessica liked her at once, whoever she was. "I'm Jessica Thorne," she extended her hand and the woman gripped it with strong fingers. Jessica noticed the large diamond wedding ring glittering against her tanned skin.

"I know," she said softly. "Could I talk with you for a few minutes?"

That puzzled Jessica a bit, then she decided the woman probably wanted to know something about Seascape.

"Certainly. How about some iced tea?"

The woman smiled. "My favorite drink. I'd love it."

As they walked up to the house, the woman began to look around and her pleasant smile widened. "My goodness, you've done a beautiful job with this place."

Jessica glanced at her. "You've been here before?"

"Well, no. But I've heard a lot about your house."

"Oh?" Jessica's curiosity mounted as they climbed the steps and the woman turned to survey the ocean.

"What a lovely view you have."

Jessica smiled quickly, following the woman's gaze to the ocean. "Yes, it is nice, isn't it? I'm sorry, I didn't catch your name."

The woman turned to look at Jessica again, and for a

moment an expression of sadness touched her features. "I'm afraid I didn't give you my name. Actually, I came to speak with you about Mark Castleman. I'm his mother."

Jessica stared, speechless.

"Could we sit down for a moment, please?"

The woman was polite and she seemed truly kind. Jessica knew it would be rude not to at least hear what she had to say. She sank into the chair and looked back at the woman, trying to imagine her married to Jack Barkley. She couldn't.

"I'm Grace, by the way. Grace Castleman."

Jessica nodded, staring at the woman's features. While she was very attractive, she bore no resemblance to Mark.

"John and I came down for Mr. Barkley's funeral," she hesitated, watching Jessica carefully. "I'd like to explain some things to you, if you'll just give me a few minutes."

Jessica didn't respond to that. She was still angry with Mark, but there was no way she could be rude to this pleasant woman.

"All right," Jessica replied, waiting.

Grace Castleman folded her hands in her lap and studied them thoughtfully for a moment. Then she looked back at Jessica.

"We adopted Mark when he was five days old."

"Adopted?" Jessica echoed.

Grace smiled gently. "That's right. His mother was Jack Barkley's second wife. I never met her, but I do know quite a lot about her. Her sister worked for an adoption agency in Birmingham. When Paulette Barkley decided she didn't want her baby, she phoned her sister. We had adopted a baby girl at that agency three years before. She was the joy of our lives, but we wanted a son to complete our family. We had been waiting for over a year when finally the call came."

Her voice softened as tears filled her eyes, but she quickly dashed a hand to her cheeks. "Forgive me. It's just that Mark and Felicia are the greatest gifts of our lives. It's amazing how God answers prayers."

Jessica was mesmerized by those words, and by the woman, as well. "Please go on," she urged her.

Grace Castleman reached into her handbag for a Kleenex and dabbed at her eyes.

"We couldn't have asked for a better son. Of course we told him that he was adopted when he was quite young. He didn't seem to think much about it until he became a teen-ager. Then he began to question me about his birth parents. I suppose we all want to know about our roots, but in Mark's case, he was really curious. Felicia never seemed to care."

She lifted her eyes, staring into space. "After all that has happened with Mr. Barkley, I see that Mark was meant to find his birth father." She looked back at Jessica, smiling. "Back to my story. When Mark graduated from college, he told us he wanted to find the people who gave birth to him. He would never think of them as parents, he assured us, but for his own peace of mind, he wanted to know."

She hesitated, staring out at the ocean. "My husband accepted that much easier than I did." She glanced back at Jessica. "As a mother, I wanted to protect him. And, selfishly, there was always the fear that he would — I don't know — like them better, I suppose." She smiled at Jessica. "I know that sounds silly, but it's just honest."

Jessica nodded. "I can understand your feelings. I think I would probably be the same way."

Grace studied her slim hands, folded in her lap. She took

a deep breath and looked back at Jessica. "We gave him the name of the adoption agency. His biological aunt still works there, although she is retiring this year. When Mark called, she told him everything." Grace sighed, studying her hands again. "His biological mother died years ago in an automobile accident in Los Angeles. She wanted to be an actress but never made it. Mr. Barkley was easy to find, and I suppose he believed Mark right from the beginning. Of course, he checked him out, which was easy to do, since Amanda — that's Mark's aunt — confirmed that Paulette was his mother. Paulette had told Mr. Barkley that she lost the baby while he was in Europe."

Jessica stared at Grace Castleman, stunned by everything she had heard. Suddenly, all the pieces to the puzzle were beginning to fall into place.

"When Mark called and told us Mr. Barkley had offered him a position in the company, John and I had a difficult time accepting this. Then Mark explained the kind of person he was — ruthless and uncaring — and that he had hurt a lot of people. Mark wanted to turn the company around, try to make amends for some of the bad things Mr. Barkley had done. And, too, the man was dying of lung cancer. We're very proud of Mark for staying on to help."

Jessica bit her lip, thinking it was the most amazing story she had ever heard. It would take awhile to sort it all out in her mind, particularly where she was concerned.

"Jessica, I've never known Mark to be dishonest or deceitful about anything in his entire life. I can't imagine why he didn't tell you the truth in the beginning."

Jessica had been staring out at the beach, thinking about that first day she met him.

"I know why. I became irate whenever the subject of Barkley came up. If he had told me he was connected to Barkley, we would never have become friends."

Grace touched her hand. "You can't possibly imagine how sorry he is for that deceit. I hope someday that you'll give him another chance."

Jessica gripped Grace's hand and smiled. "I'm afraid I'm the one who won't get a second chance. Do you know about the interview? It was very foolish of me."

Grace grinned impishly. "He's still a little angry over that, but he'll get over it." Her eyes were serious again. "He has so much responsibility with this corporation. John and I are worried that he is taking on so much, but we feel he's equal to the task."

Jessica began to nod as she imagined Mark taking over the company. She was certain he would do a good job. "I'm sure he is."

"In time, maybe you two can work things out. I know how he feels about you," she said, "even though he tries to hide it now. Mark's never been in love, so naturally I was curious about you."

In love! Jessica could hardly believe those words or that Mark had told his mother so much.

The sound of Wilma's car interrupted her thoughts, and Grace, too, was glancing toward the driveway.

"You have company, so I'll go now."

"No, please. I'd like you to stay and talk for a while. That's Wilma. She lives here and helps me. We'll be having lunch soon. Will you join us?"

Grace's blue eyes twinkled as she smiled at Jessica. "I'd love to. It's nice of you to ask me."

Looking at this remarkable woman, Jessica found it easy to understand why Mark had turned out so well. Grace Castleman seemed to be a wonderful person, and Jessica wanted to hang onto her for a while longer, get to know her better. Then suddenly she remembered the painting she had sent.

"Oh, you have to see how well your painting fits my wall!" Jessica exclaimed, hopping to her feet.

"I'd like that. Mark told me you were pleased with the painting."

"And I had intended to send a thank-you note. I'm really embarrassed that I haven't."

Grace brushed the matter aside, asking questions about the house. Soon they were both talking at once about colors and decorating ideas, and as Jessica looked at Grace and listened to her gentle voice, she liked her more than anyone she had ever met — except for Mark.

Meanwhile, Mark was standing at the airport, watching his father's plane take off. His mother and father had come down yesterday to spend the night with Mark and attend Jack's funeral. His father had already committed to a Board of Directors meeting and needed to get back to Birmingham. His mother was staying on for a few days to help him settle into the house. Since his mother had some shopping to do, he had seized the opportunity to spend another hour with his father. He valued his advice, and today Mark felt he needed a ton of it.

As the silver plane disappeared into the clouds, Mark turned from the window and hurried back through the airport. He had a dozen things to do today — meetings, paper-work, interviews. His mind began to spin whenever he tried to grasp it all at once, but his father had just advised him to make a list and attack the jobs one by one.

"Just go from number one to number two," he slapped him on the shoulder, "and delegate responsibility. I'm a master at that, remember?" His teasing remark brought a smile to Mark's face. He'd always appreciated his dad's sense of humor. It had gotten them through many difficult situations.

"I only hope I can do as well as you," Mark had said, shaking his father's hand one last time before he boarded the plane.

"You better," he grinned, "for I'll be looking over your shoulder if you're not careful."

His father had met all the staff at Barkley and had given Mark his opinions on who would remain loyal and who would not. Mark trusted his father's instincts, and he intended to follow every word of his advice.

As he reached the parking area and hurried toward the car, he spotted a slim, dark-haired woman up ahead. Something about her reminded him of Jessica. He looked away, not wanting to think of Jessica, ever again; and yet she kept popping into his thoughts. He told himself that he was being weak. He hadn't known her that long, he should be able to forget her. But he couldn't.

Again and again, he went over the interview in his mind, trying to hold onto his anger toward her. How, he asked himself, could she have said all those things?

He reached into his pocket for his car keys, thinking of last night's conversation with his mother. They had sat up late, talking about all that had happened. She had a way of drawing out of him his deepest secrets, and he had ended up telling her about Jessica.

"Mark, you should have told her the truth," she had admonished in her gentle way.

"I know. But it doesn't matter now," he had said, trying to conceal the heartache he felt. By the expression of concern on his mother's face, he doubted that he had fooled her. She knew him too well. She had tried to rationalize Jessica's actions, but Mark rallied back, refusing to see things differently.

"Why don't you just call her, talk things through?" she suggested.

"No. There's nothing to say," he replied.

His mother touched his cheek gently and smiled. "Mark Castleman, you are a very stubborn man," she teased.

He shrugged and grinned. "I know."

"Maybe things will change in time," she said lightly, easing away from the subject. Mark had always marveled at how well she could do that.

"Maybe." But he doubted that as he told himself he never wanted to see Jessica Thorne again. They had settled their debt with her; it was over.

Nineteen

Jessica turned down the main street of Angel Valley and breathed a sigh of relief. This was the one place in all the world that she could come back to and always feel at home. There was a sense of peace here, and what she needed more than anything in the world right now was peace.

She had pulled out before daybreak, leaving a note on the kitchen table for Wilma. Buying some things for Seascape gave her an excuse to come to Angel Valley, even though she couldn't haul the rockers back in her car. Still, she could make arrangements for payments, and she hoped to pick up some knickknacks at the arts and crafts center here.

She smiled to herself, looking around. It almost seemed that she had stepped back into another century after driving through busy cities on her way up to the Smokies. She glanced from the frame and concrete buildings to the park in the center of town. The few old-timers settled on the park benches were huddled into their coats, for it was a brisk winter day. They sat whittling together, chuckling over something someone had said. It did her soul good to come back to this wonderful little place nestled in the clouds, guarded by angels, as everyone liked to say.

She spotted a familiar face here and there and waved. She slowed up at the arts and crafts center, wondering if she should shop now or visit Laurel.

Visit Laurel, she decided, as she turned west and drove toward the new home Laurel had described in her last letter. She rounded a curve and spotted the new log home built on the crest of a hill, against a background of blue-hazed mountains. Large windows reflected the sunlight across a wide porch where rockers and a huge swing invited company. Jessica could imagine Laurel and Matt sitting here, enjoying the view, enjoying their life together.

As she climbed the porch steps, the door flew open and Laurel rushed out, throwing her arms around Jessica.

"Jessica! What a wonderful surprise!"

"Hey," Jessica leaned back to look at her, "something has come between us, I'd say."

Laurel rubbed the round belly protruding from her oversized sweater and stirrup pants. "Our little bundle of joy. A boy, I think, although we're not sure yet."

Jessica stared at Laurel for several seconds, thinking she had never looked prettier. Her blonde hair was pulled back in a ponytail, her eyes shone with happiness, and the glow of a natural blush touched her cheeks. She was the picture of perfect health.

"You look great, Laurel!" Jessica said, slipping her arm around Laurel's shoulder as they entered the house.

"So do you." As she closed the door, Laurel turned to face her. "I pray for you a lot, Jessica. I know it's been rough."

Jessica nodded, taking a deep breath. "Things are getting

better," she said, as her eyes traveled over the living room, done in shades of green splashed with pale gold. She had the impression of sunlight playing over a forest. "You have amazing taste," Jessica said.

"Matt's the one with the decorating sense. He's great at this. And all our furniture is handmade, from the arts and crafts center."

Jessica nodded, looking from intricately carved tables and chairs to massive sofas, and finally lovely oil paintings hanging on the walls. She recognized afghans and quilts made by folks in the valley, and everything fit together perfectly, creating a wonderful home for Matt and Laurel.

"It's beautiful," she said, turning back to Laurel. "When I leave here, I'm going back by the center and pick up a few things, then on to Harold's for some rockers."

"Great. But you won't get to see Matt, I'm sorry to say. He's in Knoxville today. Hey, you have to spend the night. I won't take no for an answer, so come on in and we'll have tea and catch up on conversation."

"A deal," Jessica smiled, following Laurel back to the kitchen. Along the way she spotted more of the handmade items that Matt and Laurel were marketing across the country. "Laurel, you two have provided such a great service for this community." Jessica smiled at her friend as they reached the kitchen.

"And the community has done a lot for us," she called over her shoulder as she put the kettle on to heat. "Have a seat."

Jessica sat down at a round oak table with matching ladderback chairs. "Who made this?"

"Harold! We convinced him if he could build rockers he

could build tables. Of course, he has several of the local men working for him now. You should get one of these tables."

"I'd love to," Jessica replied, running her hand over the smooth grain of the wood.

"So tell me what's going on," Laurel said, turning sideways to fit herself into a chair at the table.

Jessica looked at Laurel's round belly and grinned. She had never seen a pregnant woman look so good, or so happy. She pushed her thoughts back to the question Laurel had asked.

"The B&B will open in another week, if I'm lucky. But before I tell you about that, there's something else." She took a deep breath. "I've met someone."

Laurel placed her elbows on the table and leaned forward. "I'm all ears."

Jessica bit her lip, trying to think where to begin. She decided to start with Blake's deception, and as she talked it was as though a wound that had been festering for a long time was being lanced and the infection was draining out. She talked for an hour, scarcely noticing when Laurel got up and filled the cups, then filled them again. Laurel had always been a good listener, but Jessica had forgotten how important that was until she told her story, prompted by Laurel's nods and an occasional question. Finally, when she had told everything, particularly Mark's role in her life, Laurel reached across the table and gripped her hand.

"It's going to work out, Jessica. I know that. I can feel it in my spirit."

Jessica tilted her head and looked at Laurel, wishing desperately that she could believe that. "I don't see how," she finally answered. "Mark is angry with me, and he has every reason to be. And I can't bring myself to go see him and apologize. I've tried, but I just can't." She hesitated, thinking about her life. "You know, Laurel, I've just had this terrible problem with forgiveness. I can't seem to forgive people for what they've done to me.

"Then let me give you some verses to think about," Laurel answered. "The verses come from the sixth chapter of Luke.

"'Do not judge, and you will not be judged. Do not condemn, and you will not be condemned. Forgive, and you will be forgiven. For with the measure you use, it will be measured to you.'"

"Those are nice words," Jessica said, "but I can't imagine asking people who have hurt me to forgive me for retaliating."

"I know. Forgiveness is never simple. I've learned that, but I promise you when you carry a grudge, the person you hurt most is yourself."

Jessica nodded. "So if I forgive people like Jack Barkley, Mark, even Blake, then I can expect to be forgiven and to find peace at last. Is that what you think the verse means?"

"That's what I think it means," Laurel answered softly.

Jessica frowned. "Laurel, I don't know if Mark will ever forgive me for granting that interview. What bothers me most is the fact that the paper came out the day before Jack Barkley died. Mr. Barkley might have read the story."

She dropped her eyes, feeling sad again. "No matter what the man had done, I can't bear to think that something I said might have hastened his death." Her shoulders slumped beneath the weight of that possibility. She had hated him so much. Now she had her revenge, if she wanted to look at it that way.

Laurel got up and came around the table, her round belly leading the way, but she didn't seem hampered by the extra weight. She put her arms around Jessica's shoulders and gave her a warm hug.

"Let go and let God. He can heal those places in your heart, and in the hearts of others as well. Trust him. That's the only way anything can ever work."

"I think you're right." Jessica hugged Laurel tighter. "It means so much to have a friend like you. I've been so confused, so lonely."

They held each other for another few seconds, then suddenly a jab against Jessica's shoulder sent Laurel into a fit of laughter. "I guess he's jealous!" she said, stepping back from Jessica to rub her stomach. "Little Matt is a bit possessive right now."

Jessica began to laugh too, and as their laughter grew, it occurred to Jessica that this was the first time she had felt really good since before her breakup with Mark.

After spending the night with Laurel and Matt, Jessica left town, loaded down with items she had bought in Angel Valley. She and Laurel had gone to visit Granny and she had left with armloads of honey and homemade jellies and jams. Granny refused payment, saying it was her little gift to Seascape. A truck from the arts and crafts center would deliver the rockers later in the week.

Before leaving Angel Valley, Jessica drove to the end of town and turned into the parking lot of the white clapboard community church. There were no cars around — the pastor was probably out on a visit. She cut the engine and got out, walking slowly up the front steps.

The tears in her eyes slipped down her cheeks as she

recalled her wedding here, almost a year ago; yet it seemed much longer. So much had happened since then. While most towns were now forced to lock their church doors, she knew as she touched the handle this door would be unlocked, and it was.

The interior was dim, yet the red carpet that stretched from the door to the pulpit welcomed her. She made her way past the empty oak pews, recalling Sunday mornings when everyone sang merrily to the old hymns. Reaching the altar, she knelt and looked up at the wooden cross. It was then, in the sacred quiet of the church, that she gave way to the racking sobs and voiced her own private prayer. She wanted to be cleansed and healed of her anger and bitterness, and she wanted the strength and the grace to forgive — to let go and let God, as Laurel had said.

She knelt there for several minutes, waiting for a sense of peace to wash over her. And it did. A new strength began to fill her and she stood again, wiping her cheeks. She had done what she could to make things right between herself and God; now it was up to him to take care of the rest.

Mark sat at the end of the polished mahogany table, facing his board of directors. He had outlined his plans now, argued down one vehement objection, appeased a few more doubtful faces, and was about to conclude the meeting.

"So you really think that in the long run refinancing all the delinquent mortgages is the answer?" Walter asked.

"It's what I want to do," Mark replied firmly. "We're building a new image for this company. If anyone doesn't agree with this policy, I'm willing to discuss matters further in the privacy of my office. Meanwhile, I think we've spent enough time going over the pros and cons. It's time to get to work."

A full minute of silence followed, then suddenly everyone was coming to their feet, breathing sighs of relief. Mark scooped up his folders and hurried back to the office, glad the worst was over.

Jessica sat at her desk, studying her register. Her first guests, the Spencers, were from Atlanta. Mrs. Spencer had called to make reservations, saying she and her husband came to Florida every spring. They had booked with her for the entire week. Jessica suspected that her father was somehow responsible for this reservation, when she noticed Mr. Spencer's place of employment. It was the same pharmaceutical company for which her father worked, and while the company had offices in several states, she doubted this was a coincidence.

"Thanks, Dad," she grinned, stretching her arms over her head.

She had been at her desk for hours; she only had one more afternoon for relaxing before her long work days began. She got out of her chair and wandered to the front porch where Wilma sat with Clarence, drinking coffee, listening to one of his stories.

As she stepped onto the porch, they both turned to her with wide smiles on their faces. Jessica could see they were having a good time together, and she began to wonder if something serious might not come out of this relationship.

"Join us for coffee," Wilma invited.

"Thanks, but you know I'm not a coffee drinker.

Clarence, I want to thank you again for all your hard work."

He gave her a crooked grin. "Glad to have a part in dressing up this place. Could I ask a favor?" His eyes slid to Wilma and they both grinned.

Jessica looked at Wilma, wondering what was up. "I guess so," she replied uncertainly.

"I sing in a quartet, and tonight we're having a little singing at the church. I'd be proud for you and Wilma to come."

Jessica hesitated, feeling put on the spot. She wanted to make an excuse, but both faces were looking at her expectantly and she just couldn't find a way to refuse. And besides, she had enjoyed being at the little church in Angel Valley; it had made her aware of her yearning to return to church.

"Sure. We'll come, won't we, Wilma?"

Wilma nodded eagerly, looking back at Clarence. "Just give us directions on how to get there."

Clarence went into a lengthy explanation, but Jessica had already figured out where the church was located. She kept wanting to hurry Clarence up whenever he began a conversation, but Wilma didn't seem to mind.

"We'll be there," she smiled. "And now I'm going to stretch my legs and take a walk down the beach."

"I'll catch the phone," Wilma offered then turned back to Clarence who immediately resumed his story.

As the day's sunshine spilled over her, Jessica tilted her head back, accepting its warm rays. The beach was already getting the first of the season's crowd at the condominium complex closest to her. She could see a couple tossing a beach ball to two small children, and she thought of Laurel and Matt and the baby they were expecting in September.

Jessica felt a twinge of sadness when she thought of her own life. Would she ever marry and have children?

She ended up at the water's edge, staring out at the ocean. The waves were gentle today, rolling lazily into shore.

At the moment, her life was calm and peaceful, like the waves on the ocean, but she had learned that without warning, everything could change. The waters could become rough and frightening.

She was still troubled by all that had happened, but her trip to Angel Valley had changed her life. Time spent with dear friends, followed up by a trip to church and a quiet earnest prayer, had given her a new lease on life.

Forgive and forget. It had been difficult until she stepped inside the little church in Angel Valley. That sense of peace had remained with her, and although she still worried about the future, she felt much better about her life.

She thought of Grace Castleman. She was such a gracious woman, so kind and caring. She had told her that when she returned to Birmingham, she would start making preparations for the mission trip she and her husband planned to take in early summer. This year they were going to Guatemala.

Jessica had politely questioned her, aware she wanted to talk about the trip. In the back of her mind, she kept pondering their willingness to take off every summer for some remote place to help perfect strangers. From what Grace had told her, they worked hard building a church or repairing homes in impoverished areas. In doing so, they served as missionaries, spreading the gospel.

"It's the best time we have all year," she had told her.

Jessica frowned, slipping her hands into the pockets of her jeans, watching a seagull dip and sway over the water. She was learning a valuable lesson through this season of hardship, and it had to do with priorities and commitment to the right goals.

At last her self-confidence had been strengthened; she hadn't been wrong about Mark, after all.

Jessica and Wilma sat in the oak pews of the small church that evening, listening to the old hymns brought to fever pitch in the strong exuberant voices of the men in the quartet. Jessica had tried to conceal to Wilma how much she dreaded this evening, but to her surprise she was actually enjoying herself.

Her eyes slipped over the other people who were tapping their feet or nodding their heads in time to the music. Everyone seemed happy and relaxed. She looked at Clarence. His head was tilted back as he sang out in deep bass. It was a hymn about love for one's neighbor. She found herself thinking of the words, and the many verses Clarence had quoted.

She smiled as she looked at him. He was a simple little man who drove a battered green truck and found joy in painting other people's houses. Yet, he was such a happy man, at peace with himself, loving his neighbor. She found herself comparing him to J. C. Barkley who had so much and yet so little. There was a valuable lesson to be learned here, she realized, if she would see it and take it to heart.

Everyone was invited to join in on the chorus and Jessica did, feeling shy at first, then slowly releasing herself to the music. She suddenly realized how much she had missed singing church songs.

Mark had invited her to church twice, and she had refused both times. If she had gone with him, would she have felt this warmth in her heart? Would she have prayed for God to cleanse her angry, unforgiving spirit? If she had, things might have turned out differently.

She dropped her eyes to her hands, clutched tightly in her lap. Why had she been so stubborn about coming back to God? She had forgotten how good it felt to be in God's house, singing hymns, thinking of Scripture.

It occurred to her now that one of the reasons she had been so happy in Angel Valley was because her lifestyle was centered on the little church and its activities.

Blake never attended church, although he claimed to be a Christian, and she had lapsed into the habit of skipping church as well. Then it became easy to find fault with Christians, and everyone else. And she had been an easy prey for other bad habits as well — carrying grudges, being critical and unforgiving.

Wilma was whispering something to her, and she turned, startled.

"What did you say?" she whispered back.

"There's an ice cream social afterwards. Want to stay?"

Jessica smiled. "Of course."

Later, everyone milled around the church basement, eating homemade ice cream and exchanging pleasantries. Everyone was interested in hearing about her bed and breakfast, and she enjoyed telling them.

"Clarence, I had a wonderful time," she said, as he walked Jessica and Wilma back to the car.

"Then why don't you and Wilma come back on Sunday?"

She smiled. "We just may do that."

"When tourist season starts, it may be difficult," Wilma reminded her.

"Then come in the evening," Clarence suggested. "The service starts at seven."

Jessica nodded, glancing at Wilma. "We'll work something out."

They drove home humming the songs they had heard, and as Jessica turned in to her driveway, she was amazed at how much better she felt.

"Wilma, when I was up at Angel Valley I went back to my church there. I asked God to cleanse me of this unforgiving spirit, and to heal any hurts I've caused others." She glanced at Wilma over the lights of the dashboard. "I feel so much better."

"I'm glad. Now God can make things right in your life."

"You know, Wilma, I wonder now why it's been such a problem for me."

"Because we're only human, that's why. I've been quite perturbed with Robin over the years, not to the point of being unforgiving with her, but I'm plenty angry because she can't seem to find herself."

Jessica set the brake and cut the engine. "Give her time. Maybe that trip back into frontier country will squelch her restless spirit. I bet she'll be glad to settle down someplace next year."

Wilma sighed. "I hope so."

Twenty

M om, I can't believe you did that!"

Mark stormed around the kitchen while his mother sat quietly at the breakfast table, after telling him about meeting Jessica.

"Mark," she smiled, "I love you dearly, but I repeat — you are a very stubborn man."

"If I'm stubborn, what is Jessica Thorne?"

Grace laughed softly. "She's a bit stubborn too, I suppose. Or maybe you just need to have a talk. Then you would find out that neither of you is very stubborn when it comes to matters of the heart. If you care for this girl as much as you say, it's worth a second try, don't you think?"

Mark stopped his pacing in the center of the kitchen floor and raked a hand through his hair. He was still in pajamas with his bacon and eggs getting cold on the plate. He heaved a sigh, thrust his hands on his hips and glanced across the room at the woman he respected more than anyone.

"I have all I can handle right now, Mom."

Her eyes were instantly filled with compassion as she

began to nod. "I know you do, darling." She looked around the huge kitchen, finding it cold and impersonal. She hated to return to Birmingham and leave Mark with so many choices to make. "Have you considered staying on at the condo, rather than moving in here? This house gives me the creeps."

Mark's green eyes drifted toward the arched doorway leading into the formal dining room, a very, very formal dining room.

"I don't know what I'm going to do. I'm not ready to sell the house yet."

"No, of course not. You should take plenty of time to consider every decision you make. It's just that this place isn't you — unless you want to redecorate completely. I suppose you could turn that over to a decorator, and I could come back and help out."

Mark shrugged. "I have to keep my mind on the business right now. It's going to be a daylight-to-dark ordeal for the next few weeks."

She got up and walked across the room. "I know it is, darling, but I want you to know how proud your father and I are. And we're confident you can turn that business around and make it into something worthwhile, a company that can reflect your wonderful Christian spirit."

He gave her a wry grin. "Do you think a company can do that?"

"Of course I do! Remember the Christian businessmen's group your father joined years ago?"

He nodded, recalling dinner conversations when his father had revealed some fine things that were being done by companies to help underprivileged and disabled people.

"Yes, that's why I have a vague hope that something can be accomplished here."

"I'm certain it can. Now come eat your breakfast. I'll put your plate in the microwave for a few minutes while you try to find that appetite I stole with the mention of —" She broke off. "Try to stoke up that appetite again, hon."

Mark took a seat, looking thoughtfully out the window for several seconds. When Grace set his breakfast before him again, he reached out, touching her hand.

"Thanks for everything you've done. I don't mean to sound ungrateful."

"You didn't," she smiled, taking a seat. "You were merely being honest."

"And stubborn. You're right about that." He sighed. "I don't know, Mom. It's just that I never felt about any girl the way I feel about Jessica."

Grace smiled gently at him. Of course she already knew that, but if he wanted to talk she was more than willing to listen.

"I should have told her the truth in the beginning, but she was so angry at Jack...." He shrugged and picked up a fork. "I kept thinking there would be a better time, but I realize now I was only being a coward about it. I should have known there was never going to be a right time."

"Well, we all make mistakes, Mark. You meant well. And I think she realizes that now." She hesitated, wondering if she should say more. She waited until he had taken a few bites of his breakfast then decided to go on and say it.

"I really liked her. I think she is a very brave young lady. And very sweet."

He nodded slowly. "You're right. I'm just disappointed in

her for giving that interview."

"Mark, do you think she wasn't disappointed in you when you deceived her?"

"Mom, you're killing my appetite, you know that?"

She laughed, coming to her feet. "Heaven forbid that I should do such a thing." She walked across to the cabinet to pick up her empty cup. "Want more coffee?"

"No, I'm too wired already."

"Okay, then our discussion is closed. Wait, one more thing."

He turned in his seat, giving her a wry grin. "I'll settle for just one, that's all."

"While we're on the subject of recognizing that everyone is human, I feel such sadness when I look at that portrait of Mr. Barkley." Her eyes drifted toward the den as she thought of the stern face there.

"He was not a happy man," Mark sighed.

"And the funeral —" Grace shook her head, still surprised by how few people had attended.

"The only people there were the top brass from the company plus a few businessmen who felt an obligation to come."

Grace stared into space, scarcely able to believe all that had happened to Mark, and to them as a result, upon learning of his biological father.

"Mark, could I ask you something?"

"Sure," he was buttering a biscuit.

"Are you glad you looked him up?"

Mark chewed on the biscuit, staring into space for several seconds. "In the beginning, I found myself wishing I had never pursued it. I was so disappointed to find out who he was, what he was." He leaned back in the chair, pushing his plate aside. "Then it became apparent to me that I was meant to find him. I told you what happened before he died."

Tears filled Grace's eyes. Mark had accomplished even more with the man than with the company, if possible. "I know. It's amazing that it's never too late to save someone, isn't it, Mark? Even with a last dying breath, a person can reach out to God and be accepted."

Silence filled the kitchen as both thought about the impact of that last hour Mark had spent with Jack. Then Mark looked at his mother.

"You had a hand in it, you know? It was the audio tapes you gave me that won him over."

Grace sniffled, looking for a napkin to wipe her eyes. "Isn't it amazing how God can take a simple action — my giving you the tapes — and use those tapes in such a powerful way?"

Mark nodded, thinking about that. And he was also thinking that one more effort on his part might be all it took to bridge the gap between Jessica and himself.

Jessica sat at her phone, jotting down information on a reservation card.

"Yes, Mrs. Browning, I have you down for the second weekend in April. And the Spencers referred us to you? Great. I enjoyed having them here. I'm glad to hear they had a good time."

As she finished her conversation and hung up, a smug smile sat on her lips. She knew the best advertising was by word of mouth, specifically from happy guests. It was wonderful to know that within a week, she was already getting business as a result of the nice people who had come on the weekend.

She hurried back to the kitchen to make last-minute preparations for tomorrow's guests. Wilma was busily whipping up one of her raspberry lime pies, which had been a smash hit with the Spencers.

"Wilma, I can't believe how well things are going!"

Wilma glanced across the kitchen to Jessica, pleased to see the young woman looking relaxed and happy.

"Your hard work is starting to pay off, my dear."

Jessica nodded, lifting the lid on the Dutch oven to check her latest project.

"The gumbo looks fine," she said, dipping a wooden spoon into it for a tiny sample. "Mmmm, Wilma, it's perfect."

"I didn't have any doubts. Why don't you go up and take a little nap? We have a couple of hours before the guests arrive."

Jessica replaced the lid and peered into the dining room. The table was set, everything was ready.

"I'm too wired to take a nap, but I would like a long walk on the beach. That relaxes me more than anything."

"Fine, do that."

Jessica sailed out of the house and down to the beach. The ocean breeze wafted over her, cooling her warm cheeks. She took a deep breath, touching her tongue to her lips, savoring the salty taste of the ocean. Her eyes scanned the shoreline, stretching like a white satin ribbon into the distance. Down the beach, she could see a father and son, flying an orange kite.

She found herself thinking of Mark and his adoptive parents, comparing them to Jack Barkley. This was another reason she was pro-life. A wonderful couple had been blessed by a child that Paulette chose not to keep. As she thought about the Castlemans, Jessica's legs stretched into a comfortable jog. She had taken to jogging rather than walking, since meeting Mark.

Her tennis shoes pounded into the sand, and she pumped her elbows, hoping to loosen the tension building in her body.

Ever since her return from Angel Valley, she had felt a strong urge to call Mark. She had dialed his number twice, then hung up before there was an answer. Her need to see him grew stronger every day. Somehow she had to find a way.

Mark had left the office feeling good for the first time in days. There had been a series of meetings, of course, with strong arguments against all the changes he was proposing. In the end, perseverance, determination, and prayer had won out. The interest rates of the Barkley Corporation were now the same as other lending institutions; furthermore — and this had been the hard part — he had refinanced all clients having difficulty meeting their monthly payments.

He drove along, exhausted yet contented, guiding his white Corvette toward the beach. Despite his mother's advice before leaving, he had been unable to do anything about the huge house, which felt empty and depressing to him. Since he left at daybreak and dragged back in time to collapse in bed, there had been little time to worry about how he felt in the few hours he stayed there.

Tonight was going to be different. He was driving to the

condo to escape the phone calls that trailed him everywhere. He was even paged and beeped and confronted in restaurants and restrooms. It was exhausting.

Few people knew about his place at the beach, however, and as he thought of taking a relaxing run along the shoreline, the idea was sheer heaven to him.

He rolled down the car window, inhaling deeply of the salty air. It was a pleasant afternoon, not yet six o'clock. There was plenty of time for a run on the beach, then a relaxing meal at one of his favorite restaurants.

As he reached the familiar Y in the road and turned right, he looked down the highway that led to Jessica's house. Seascape. He had practically worn out his mind thinking of her and trying to devise ways to see her again. None seemed right. In fact, he didn't seem to know what to do about the situation.

A cynical grin tilted his lips. He had gone nose to nose with attorneys, accountants, and board members all week. And he had held his own with them. Yet one delicate little woman with dark eyes and a shy smile had him completely baffled about his next move.

Some voice in his head kept telling him they needed to talk. But how? Even if their anger had cooled off, there was still the matter of pride. He was working on that. He felt good about her mortgage being cancelled by Jack. And she had dropped the lawsuit. Would that be the end of it? Would he see her again? He felt deep in his soul that he should call her once again. Just one more time. If she hung up this time, then it would be over. Forever.

As he turned into the driveway of the condo, he could already feel the taut set of his shoulders began to relax. He pulled into a parking space and cut the engine. He sat there for a moment, his eyes closed, as he took a deep breath and released it slowly. In the distance, he could hear the rhythmic pulse of the ocean, and it soothed his nerves.

He opened his eyes and got out of the car, eager to hit the beach. Sidestepping the elevator for the stairs, he took them two at a time, needing the exercise. Only slightly out of breath, he reached for his door key. He had lost seven pounds in the last two weeks, and his appetite had vanished. This place was like a miracle cure for him. He expected to be feeling much better by the time he drove back to town in the morning.

He entered the condo, yanking his shirt from his trousers, walking quickly to the large bedroom. Hurriedly, he changed clothes, pulling on his jogging suit, then laying out his bathing suit. After a jog, he'd head to the whirlpool and let the jet spray work its magic.

His eyes fell to the phone on the night stand. Again, he felt the temptation to call her. Slowly, he walked to the bed and sat down, staring at the white telephone. What would he say? That his mother had enjoyed her visit? That he thought dinner together might be a good idea?

He reached out, then hesitated. The memory of that last phone call continued to haunt him. He could still hear the sharp click in his ear, feel the sting of rejection. He hated being rejected. In fact, no woman had ever rejected him the way Jessica Thorne Vandercamp had.

There. Repeating her married name in his mind helped to distance her a bit. And, as always, he reminded himself of the newspaper article.

"A cheap shot," he muttered to himself as he got up from

the bed and charged out of the room, ready to hit the beach. He'd try for three miles today.

Jessica could see Mark's high-rise in the distance and she stopped jogging and turned toward the shoreline. She leaned over, placing her hands on her knees, trying to catch her breath.

Her chest was tight from the long jog, but she felt exhilarated and free of tension. She straightened slowly, allowing the late afternoon breeze to caress her hair, cool her face. Sunbathers were scattered about but the beach was not crowded since this was a weekday.

As her breathing became even again, she turned and cast another glance toward Mark's condominium. He was no longer here, he stayed in town now. She had read a follow-up article on the Barkley Corporation, detailing how Mark had launched some community projects to benefit the underprivileged. One project which sounded especially nice was a summer camp for handicapped children.

She was scarcely aware that she was walking toward his condominium, but when she realized that it was only thirty yards away she decided it didn't matter. She wasn't likely to see him unless he came to escape the crowds. He probably hadn't…

She squinted into the sunshine, wishing she had brought her sunglasses. There was a man, kneeling in the sand, looking at something. She blinked. Her eyes had lingered on every tall man with blond-brown hair for weeks now, but none of those men ever turned out to be Mark.

She blinked again, squinting as she drew closer to the

man. Although he had stooped to examine something there in the sand, she could see he was tall, well-toned, and…

It was Mark! She was sure of it. She lurched to a stop, her heart racing. She continued to stare at his back, wondering if she was wrong, but there was no doubt.

What should she do?

Twenty-One

Suddenly she was thinking of the day they had first met. So many times, in her hurt and anger, she had told herself he had staged their meeting. Since going to Angel Valley, talking with Laurel and praying in church, she felt less harsh. She began to walk toward him, wanting to discover the truth about him now.

She stood only a few feet away from him. He was still kneeling, studying a huge seashell that had been deposited by the tide. She bit her lip, unsure what to say to him. Then the words came to her.

"Have you lost something?" she asked.

Mark's head spun around. A look of surprise filled his eyes as he came to his feet, looking at her, making no response to her question.

Mark stared at her, unable to believe his eyes. So many times lately he had wondered how he would feel about her when he saw her again. After the newspaper interview, he had been furious with her; slowly the anger had mellowed to disappointment. He had hoped his stubborn nature would help to heal his broken heart, but eventually he had turned to praying about the matter. He wondered why he had waited so long to do that.

For here she was, standing before him, asking him the same question he had asked her weeks before.

His eyes ran up and down her slim figure. Had he lost something? He realized now, looking into those dark eyes, the delicately up-tilted face, exactly how much he had lost.

"Yes, I have. Jessica, you have to listen to me. You have to give me a chance to explain."

She said nothing. She merely stood very still, looking at him, obviously waiting for him to say more.

"I didn't intentionally deceive you. I just delayed telling you what I knew would hurt you."

She felt a stirring of the anger she had harbored, yet it was a mere twinge now.

"You should have let me be the judge of that," she said quietly. "It was unfair, Mark. You deceived me."

"Yes, I did. But was it fair for you to hang up on me without giving me a chance to explain? Was it fair to air your grievances in a newspaper article?"

She took a deep breath, thinking that he had spoken the truth. "I was angry and hurt," she answered softly.

"Mark, I am so sorry for…everything. I'm sorry for that terrible interview done in a fit of anger. And I'm sorry for the unfair way I judged you."

Seeing the sorrow in her eyes and hearing the sincerity in her voice, Mark could not stay angry. There was a quality about her that always inspired protectiveness in him. Perhaps God had given him a glimpse of her soul from the very beginning.

He found himself rushing to her defense now, wanting to bridge the gap that had separated them for too long.

He took a step closer. So did she.

"So much has happened to us," he said quietly. He thought of Jack Barkley and his problems, then Jessica and the husband who had drowned, then all the frustration she had experienced as a result of Jack Barkley. "I've prayed that somehow we could work through it, come out stronger. You've been through a lot, Jessica."

She took a deep breath, looking into his face, thinking of his problems as well as her own. "So have you. It must have been difficult searching for and finding your biological father."

He nodded. "It was. And I was so disappointed when —" He broke off, looking away. "Then I realized he was a man with a soul worth saving, that somewhere in his tough makeup there was kindness."

He took a deep breath and looked into her eyes. She was listening intently, the dark eyes soft and caring. He remembered the morning with the twins, when she had looked so natural with Molly on her hip. And he had known then he would want a woman like Jessica — maybe even Jessica herself — to be the mother of his children.

"Then I met the kind of woman I had always wanted. Only there was a big problem. Once you discovered that Jack Barkley was my biological father, I felt sure I would lose you. I ended up losing you anyway."

Looking at him now, she saw the Mark she had always known, deep in her heart. Here was the man who had brought her roses, listened to her plans for Seascape and treated her better than any man ever had. Mark was a kind and caring person. She knew what he had done for Jack Barkley and for the company. And she knew in his relationship with her he had not meant to be unfair.

Jessica knew this was the man she wanted. She had been right about him all along. She desperately hoped there was still a chance for them. Tears filled her eyes. "No, you didn't lose me."

"I didn't?"

He took a step closer. So did she.

Jessica's arms slipped around his waist. "No."

His arms encircled her, pulling her close to his chest as he searched for the right thing to say. He sighed, enjoying the luxury of having her back in his arms again.

"Mark?" She pressed her head against his chest, "I'm sorry about...Mr. Barkley."

He pulled her tighter, pressing his cheek against her soft hair, breathing the smell of her perfume. Then he began to speak, saying to her what he had told nobody else. "You know, Jessica, I cared more for him than I thought."

Jessica heard the gentleness in his voice, and she felt the pain, as well. They had both been through so much, yet somehow they had found each other again.

"I know, Mark." She took a deep breath, swallowing against the sudden ache in her throat. "I think I understand exactly how you must be feeling. As bitter as I was toward Blake, I was deeply hurt by his death."

He put his hands on her shoulders and leaned back to look down into her eyes. "Jessica, I have so many things to say to you."

"And I to you," she said, smiling through her tears.

He lifted his hands to cup her face, as his thumbs wiped

away the tears sliding down her cheeks.

"I love you. You know that, don't you?"

She pressed her cheek against his broad hand, feeling the strength there. "And I love you too," she smiled up at him.

He lowered his lips to hers, kissing her gently at first. Then as she responded to him, the kiss deepened and soon they were breathless with emotion.

For a moment they were oblivious to the people passing up and down the beach, casting amused glances in their direction. One elderly couple stopped and gawked for a few seconds, then turned to each other with an understanding smile. After all, this was the beach, and love seemed to blossom here.

Then a giggle from somewhere behind them brought Jessica back to her senses and gently she pulled away from Mark, glancing around her. When she saw the people watching in amusement, she turned her back on the crowd and smiled up at Mark.

"Why don't you come home with me?" she asked. "I think we need some privacy."

Mark nodded, slipping his arm around her waist as they began to walk down the beach, passing a couple with two small children, laughing and playing in the waves. Seagulls dipped and swayed over the sparkling green waters, and out on the horizon, the sun was slowly sinking, bathing the world in a raspberry glow.

The happy voices from the beach faded in the distance as Mark and Jessica reached the gate to Seascape. They looked back over their shoulders, admiring the view for a few more minutes. Then Mark opened the gate and they climbed the steps to the house.

Around them another spring day was coming to an end, but for Mark and Jessica this was only the beginning.

Together they would build a new and wonderful life at Seascape.

⚜

WATCH FOR: *SUNDANCE*

Follow Robin Grayson to the wilds of British Columbia, Canada, where she meets Craig Cameron, a widowed rancher with two small sons who desperately need a mother. Is Robin, free-spirited and adventurous, ready to settle down to frontier living with Craig and his two mischievous sons? Can Craig risk his heart again, while wondering if Robin can handle his rugged lifestyle? Those answers must come from God during a season of love and fear in the heart of the wilderness.

Dear Reader:

When I finished writing *Angel Valley*, I knew I wasn't ready to close the book on that wonderful little community. Jessica's character lingered in my mind, and I worried that she, like many others, had jumped into a marriage without really knowing Blake. I was curious about what would happen once they moved to Florida to open their bed and breakfast. Since my husband and I often vacation in the Florida panhandle, I was quite familiar with the white sandy beaches and emerald gulf. On our last trip there, I decided I *had* to put Jessica in that setting and tell her story.

So, as I walked the beach at sunset and thought about the best story for Jessica, the plot came to me and I couldn't imagine writing it any other way. Mark seemed like the natural hero for *Seascape,* but I wanted to show his struggle and growth as well. Other characters stepped into the story and before I knew it I was deep into my second novel for Palisades. I realized the important lesson for all the characters in *Seascape* was one of forgiveness. In writing the novel, I learned a bit more about forgiveness and I hope it may help some of you as well.

I truly enjoy my rapport with readers and love the way you have responded to Palisades. May God richly bless each and every one of you…and keep on reading!

Love,

Peggy Darty

Write to Peggy Darty: c/o Palisades
P.O.Box 1720, Sisters, Oregon 97759

PALISADES...PURE ROMANCE

THE PALISADES LINE

Ask for them at your local bookstore. If the title you seek is not in stock, the store may order you a copy using the ISBN listed.

Reunion, Karen Ball (July, 1996)
ISBN 0-88070-951-0

There are wolves on Taylor Sorensen's ranch. Wildlife biologist Connor Alexander is sure of it. So he takes a job as a ranch hand to prove it. Soon he and Taylor are caught in a fierce controversy—and in a determined battle against the growing attraction between them...an attraction that neither can ignore.

Chosen, Lisa Tawn Bergren
ISBN 0-88070-768-2

When biblical archeologist Alexsana Rourke is handed the unprecedented honor of excavating Solomon's Stables in Jerusalem, she has no idea that she'll need to rely heavily upon the new man in her life—CNN correspondent Ridge McIntyre—and God, to save her.

Refuge, Lisa Tawn Bergren
ISBN 0-88070-875-1 (New)

Part One: A Montana rancher and a San Francisco marketing exec—only one incredible summer and God could bring such diverse lives together. *Part Two:* Lost and alone, Emily Walker needs and wants a new home, a sense of family. Can one man lead her to the greatest Father she could ever want and a life full of love?

Firestorm, Lisa Tawn Bergren (October, 1996)
ISBN 0-88070-953-7

In the sequel to Bergren's best-selling *Refuge*, *Firestorm* tells the romantic tale of two unlikely soulmates: a woman who fears fire, and the man who loves it. Reyne Oldre wasn't always afraid, but a tragic accident one summer changed her forever. Can Reyne get beyond her fear and give her heart to smoke jumper Logan Quinn?

Torchlight, Lisa Tawn Bergren
ISBN 0-88070-806-9

When beautiful heiress Julia Rierdon returns to Maine to remodel her family's estate, she finds herself torn between the man she plans to marry and unexpected feelings for a mysterious wanderer who threatens to steal her heart.

Treasure, Lisa Tawn Bergren
ISBN 0-88070-725-9

She arrived on the Caribbean island of Robert's Foe armed with a lifelong dream—to find her ancestor's sunken ship—and yet the only man who can help her stands stubbornly in her way. Can Christina and Mitch find their way to the ship *and* to each other?

Cherish, Constance Colson
ISBN 0-88070-802-6

Recovering from the heartbreak of a failed engagement, Rose Anson seeks refuge at a resort on Singing Pines Island, where she plans to spend a peaceful summer studying and painting the spectacular scenery of international Lake of the Woods. But when a flamboyant Canadian and a big-hearted American compete for her love, the young artist must face her past—and her future. What follows is a search for the source and meaning of true love: a journey that begins in the heart and concludes in the soul.

Angel Valley, Peggy Darty
ISBN 0-88070-778-X

When teacher Laurel Hollingsworth accepts a summer tutoring position for a wealthy socialite family, she faces an enormous challenge in her young student, Anna Lee Wentworth. However, the real challenge is ahead of her: hanging on to her heart when older brother Matthew Wentworth comes to visit. Soon Laurel and Matthew find that they share a faith in God...and powerful feelings for one another. Can Laurel and Matthew find time to explore their relationship while she helps the emotionally troubled Anna Lee and fights to defend her love for the beautiful *Angel Valley*?

Seascape, Peggy Darty
ISBN 0-88070-927-8

On a pristine sugar sand beach in Florida, Jessica has a lot to reflect upon. The untimely death of her husband Blake...and the sudden entrance of a new man, distracting her from her grief. In the midst of opening a B&B, can Jessica overcome her anger and forgive the one responsible for Blake's death? Loving the mysterious new man in her life will depend upon it.

Sundance, Peggy Darty (August, 1996)
ISBN 0-88070-952-9

Follow Robin Grayson to the wilds of British Columbia, Canada, where she meets Craig Cameron, a widowed rancher with two small sons who desperately need a mother. Is free-spirited Robin ready to settle down in the 1990's last wild frontier? And can Craig risk his heart again, all the while wondering if Robin can handle his rugged lifestyle?

Love Song, Sharon Gillenwater
ISBN 0-88070-747-X

When famous country singer Andrea Carson returns to her hometown to recuperate from a life-threatening illness, she seeks nothing more than a respite from the demands of stardom that have sapped her creativity and ability to perform. It's Andi's old high school friend Wade Jamison who helps her to realize that she needs inner healing as well. As Andi's strength grows, so do her feelings for the rancher who has captured her heart. But can their relationship withstand the demands of her career? Or will their romance be as fleeting as a beautiful *Love Song*?

Antiques, Sharon Gillenwater
ISBN 0-88070-801-8

Deeply wounded by the infidelity of his wife, widower Grant Adams swore off all women—until meeting charming antiques dealer Dawn Carson. Although he is drawn to her, Grant struggles to trust again. Dawn finds herself overwhelmingly attracted to the darkly brooding cowboy, but won't marry a nonbeliever. As Grant learns more about her faith, he is touched by its impact on her life and slowly begins to trust.

Echoes, Robin Jones Gunn (June, 1996)
ISBN 0-88070-773-9

In this dramatic romance filled with humor, Lauren Phillips enters the wild, uncharted territory of the Internet on her home computer and "connects" with a man known only as "K.C." Recovering from a broken engagement and studying for her teaching credential, her correspondence with K.C. becomes the thing she enjoys most. Will their e-mail romance become a true love story when they meet face to face?

Secrets, Robin Jones Gunn
ISBN 0-88070-721-6

Seeking a new life as an English teacher in a peaceful Oregon town, Jessica tries desperately to hide the details of her identity from the community...until she falls in love. Will the past keep Jessica and Kyle apart forever?

Whispers, Robin Jones Gunn
ISBN 0-88070-755-0

Teri Moreno went to Maui eager to rekindle a romance. But when circumstances turn out to be quite different than she expects, she finds herself spending a great deal of time with a handsome, old high school crush who now works at a local resort. But the situation becomes more complicated when Teri meets Gordon, a clumsy, endearing Australian with a wild past, and both men begin to pursue her. Will Teri respond to God's gentle urgings toward true love? The answer lies in her response to the gentle *Whispers* in her heart.

Coming Home, Barbara Hicks (June, 1996)

ISBN 0-88070-945-6

Keith Castle is running from a family revelation that destroyed his world, and deeply hurt is heart. Katie Brannigan is his childhood friend who was wounded by his sudden disappearance. Together, Keith and Katie could find healing and learn that in his own timing, God manages all things for good. But can Katie bring herself to give love one more chance?

Glory, Marilyn Kok

ISBN 0-88070-754-2

To Mariel Forrest, the teaching position in Taiwan provided more than a simple escape from grief; it also offered an opportunity to deal with her feelings toward the God she once loved, but ultimately blamed for the deaths of her family. Once there, Mariel dares to ask the timeless question: "If God is good, why do we suffer?" What follows is an inspiring story of love, healing, and renewed confidence in God's goodness.

Diamonds, Shari MacDonald (September, 1996)

ISBN 0-88070-982-0

When spirited sports caster Casey Foster inherits a minor league team, she soon discovers that baseball isn't all fun and games. Soon, Casey is juggling crazy promotional events, major league expectations, and egos of players like Tucker Boyd: a pitcher who wants nothing more than to return to the major leagues...until Casey captures his heart and makes him see diamonds in a whole new way.

Forget-Me-Not, Shari MacDonald

ISBN 0-88070-769-0

Traveling to England's famed Newhaven estate to pursue an internship as a landscape architect, Hayley Buckman looked forward to making her long-held career dreams come true. But upon arrival, Hayley is quickly drawn to the estate and its mysterious inhabitants, despite a sinister warning urging her to leave. Will an endearing stranger help her solve the mystery and find love as well?

Sierra, Shari MacDonald

ISBN 0-88070-726-7

When spirited photographer Celia Randall travels to eastern California for a short-term assignment, she quickly is drawn to—and locks horns with—editor Marcus Stratton. Will lingering heartaches destroy Celia's chance at true love? Or can she find hope and healing high in the *Sierra*?

Westward, Amanda MacLean
ISBN 0-88070-751-8

Running from a desperate fate in the South toward an unknown future in the West, plantation-born artist Juliana St. Clair finds herself torn between two men, one an undercover agent with a heart of gold, the other a man with evil intentions and a smooth facade. Witness Juliana's dangerous travels toward faith and love as she follows God's lead in this powerful historical novel.

Stonehaven, Amanda MacLean
ISBN 0-88070-757-7

Picking up in the years following *Westward, Stonehaven* follows Callie St. Clair back to the South where she has returned to reclaim her ancestral home. As she works to win back the plantation, the beautiful and dauntless Callie turns it into a station on the Underground Railroad. Covering her actions by playing the role of a Southern belle, Callie risks losing Hawk, the only man she has ever loved. Readers will find themselves quickly drawn into this fast-paced novel of treachery, intrigue, spiritual discovery, and unexpected love.

Everlasting, Amanda MacLean (May, 1996)
ISBN 0-88070-929-4

Picking up where the captivating *Stonehaven* left off, *Everlasting* brings readers face to face once more with charming, courageous—and very Irish—Sheridan O'Brian. Will she find her missing twin? And will Marcus Jade, a reporter bent on finding out what really happened to Shamus, destroy his chances with her by being less than honest?

Betrayed, Lorena McCourtney
ISBN 0-88070-756-9

As part of a wealthy midwestern family, young Rosalyn Fallon was sheltered from the struggles brought on by the Depression. But after the collapse of her father's company and the elopement of her fiancé and best friend, Rosalyn unexpectedly finds herself facing both hardship and heartbreak. Will her new life out West and a man as rugged and rough as the land itself help her recover?

Escape, Lorena McCourtney (November, 1996)
ISBN 1-57673-012-3

Is money really everything? The winsome Beth Curtis must come to terms with that question as she fights to hold on to guardianship of her nephew, even facing her deceased sister-in-law's brother. Sent to collect the boy, handsome Guy Wilkerson has no idea that he will fall for Beth, and come to see his own family's ways of living in a new light. Can the two overcome such diversity to be together, beginning their own family?

***Voyage,* Elaine Schulte (August, 1996)**
ISBN 1-57673-011-5
Traveling via ship to the Holy Land, Ann Marie is on a pilgrimage, discovering things about faith and love all the way. But will a charming man who guides her—among the romantic streets of Greece and elsewhere—distract her from the One who truly loves her?

***A Christmas Joy,* MacLean, Darty, Gillenwater**
ISBN 0-88070-780-1 (same length as other Palisades books)
Snow falls, hearts change, and love prevails! In this compilation, three experienced Palisades authors spin three separate novelettes centering around the Christmas season and message:
By Amanda MacLean: A Christmas pageant coordinator in a remote mountain village of Northern California is reunited with an old friend and discovers the greatest gift of all.
By Peggy Darty: A college ski club reunion brings together model Heather Grant and an old flame. Will they gain a new understanding?
By Sharon Gillenwater: A chance meeting in an airport that neither of them could forget...and a Christmas reunion.

***Mistletoe:* Ball, Hicks, McCourtney (October, 1996)**
ISBN 1-57673-013-1
A new Christmas anthology of three novellas...all in one keepsake book!